Goals Clear Dreams

AF673741

PREFACE :-

Every great achievement begins with a clear goal and a strong dream. This book is designed to help you move from confusion to clarity, and from thinking to real action. Many people have dreams, but only a few know how to turn them into reality. The difference is not luck, it is the right mindset, discipline, and daily direction.

In this book, you will learn how to set clear goals, build powerful habits, stay focused, and overcome challenges with confidence. Each chapter gives practical guidance that you can apply in your daily life. The ideas are simple, but the impact can be life-changing when followed with consistency.

This is not just a book to read, it is a guide to follow. If you are ready to take control of your life, stay committed to your goals, and build a meaningful future, this journey will help you move forward with clarity and purpose.

Goals Clear Dreams

Author : Hargundeep Singh
Self Published By
Hargundeep Singh
Contact : 8847322194

Edition : I

Publisher

CONTENT

INTRODUCTION

In today's fast-moving world, many people feel busy but still lack clear direction in their lives. They work hard, follow routines, and chase success, yet often feel confused about where they are going and why they are doing what they do. This book, *Goals Clear Dreams*, is written to solve this problem by helping you bring clarity to your thinking and purpose to your actions. It is designed to guide you step by step in understanding what you truly want and how to achieve it with confidence and focus. Success is not only about talent or luck; it is about having a clear vision, setting meaningful goals, and taking consistent action every day. Many people have dreams, but without structure and discipline, those dreams remain only ideas. This book will help you transform your dreams into clear goals and then into daily actions that create real results. It focuses on building a strong foundation of mindset, habits, and planning so that your journey becomes practical and achievable.

A major part of success depends on how you think and how you respond to challenges. That is why this book goes deep into developing a powerful mindset. You will learn how to overcome fear, remove limiting beliefs, stay focused, and build mental strength. Life will always bring difficulties, but with the right thinking, every challenge can become an opportunity for growth. This book will help you develop resilience so that you can stay strong and continue moving forward, no matter the situation.

Time, discipline, and focus are also key elements in achieving success. Many people struggle not because they lack ability, but because they do not use their time effectively. In this book, you will learn how to manage your time, build productive habits, and stay consistent in your efforts. It will teach you how small daily actions can lead to big results when done with clarity and commitment. This approach makes success more practical and less overwhelming. Another important part of this journey is understanding purpose and fulfillment. True success is not only about achieving goals but also about living a meaningful life. This book will guide you in discovering your purpose, aligning your actions with your values, and creating a positive impact on others. It will help you build strong relationships, maintain balance in life, and find satisfaction beyond material success.

Goals Clear Dreams is more than just a book; it is a complete guide to personal growth and transformation. It is written in simple and practical language so that anyone can understand and apply its lessons. If you are ready to take control of your life, develop clarity, and turn your dreams into reality, this book will support you at every step. Your journey toward success begins with one clear decision, and this book is here to help you take that first step with confidence and purpose.

1.

THE POWER OF VISION

Understanding What Vision Means in Personal success

Daniel and Michael started working at the same company at the same time. Both were hardworking and had similar opportunities in life. In the beginning, their lives looked very similar. However, there was one important difference between them. Daniel spent time thinking about what he wanted to achieve in the future, while Michael only focused on his daily work and never thought seriously about his long-term goals.

Daniel believed that success starts with having a clear vision. He thought about the kind of career he wanted, the skills he needed to learn, and the life he hoped to build in the future. Because of this, he made careful decisions. He chose work that helped him learn new things, improved his knowledge, and slowly built his experience. His vision helped him stay focused on his future.

Michael also worked hard every day, but he did not have a clear direction. When new opportunities came, he often followed what others were doing instead of thinking about what was best for him. Sometimes he changed his plans quickly and tried different things without a clear reason. Even though he stayed busy, he often felt confused about where his life was going.

As time passed, Daniel slowly started moving forward in his career. He continued learning new skills and improving himself.

Even when work became difficult, he stayed motivated because he remembered the future he wanted to create. His clear vision helped him stay patient and keep working toward his goals.

Michael later realized that working hard alone is not always enough. Without a clear vision, people can spend many years working but still feel unsure about their direction. Vision helps people understand where they want to go and why they are working so hard.

The story of Daniel and Michael teaches an important lesson. When a person has a clear vision, their efforts become more meaningful. Vision helps people make better choices, stay focused, and move step by step toward a better future. It gives direction to hard work and helps turn effort into real progress.

The Difference Between Having Dreams and Having a Clear Vision

Many people have dreams about a better future. They may dream of success, financial freedom, a good career, or a happy life. Dreams are important because they inspire hope and positive thinking. They allow people to imagine what their life could become. However, dreams are often general and not clearly defined. A person may say they want to become successful, but they may not know exactly how to achieve it or what steps they should take. Because of this, many dreams remain only in the mind and never become reality.

A clear vision is different from a simple dream. Vision gives direction to a dream. When a person develops a clear vision, they start understanding what they truly want and why it is important for their life. Vision makes a person think seriously about their future. Instead of only wishing for success, they begin to plan how they will reach their goals. Vision brings clarity and purpose to their thoughts.

For example, a person may dream of becoming financially strong.

This is a common dream, but it is still very broad. When this dream becomes a vision, the person starts thinking more clearly. They may decide to learn new skills, start a business, improve their career, or manage their money better. Vision turns a general dream into a practical path that a person can follow step by step.

Another important difference is that dreams stay mostly in imagination, while vision encourages action. When people have a clear vision, they start taking responsibility for their future. They begin to plan their time, improve their knowledge, and work with focus. Vision pushes a person to take small but meaningful steps every day. These small steps slowly create real progress in life.

Vision also helps people stay strong during difficult situations. In life, challenges and failures are normal. If a person only has dreams, they may lose motivation when problems appear. But when someone has a clear vision, they remember their purpose and keep moving forward. Vision gives mental strength and patience during tough times.

Understanding the difference between dreams and vision can change the way a person thinks about life. Dreams show what is possible, but vision shows how it can be achieved. When people turn their dreams into a clear vision, they stop only hoping for a better future and start building it through their actions and decisions.

How Vision Shapes Long-Term Life Decisions

Vision plays an important role in shaping long-term life decisions because it gives a person a clear direction for the future. When someone has a strong vision, they understand what kind of life they want to build and what goals they want to achieve. Because of this clarity, they start making decisions that support their future instead of only thinking about short-term comfort. Vision helps a person stay focused on what truly matters in life.

When people do not have a clear vision, their decisions are often based on temporary situations or the opinions of others. They may change their path many times because they are unsure about what they really want. This can lead to confusion and wasted effort. On the other hand, a person with vision thinks carefully before making important choices such as career decisions, education, financial planning, and personal growth.

Vision also helps people choose opportunities wisely. In life, many opportunities appear, but not all of them lead to meaningful progress. When someone has a clear vision, they can evaluate whether an opportunity supports their long-term goals or distracts them from their path. This ability to choose wisely saves time and energy and helps a person stay on the right track.

Another important benefit of vision is that it builds patience and discipline. Long-term success often requires consistent effort and the ability to delay short-term pleasures. When people clearly understand their future goals, they are more willing to work hard, learn new skills, and stay committed even when results take time. Vision reminds them why their efforts are important.

Vision also reduces confusion during difficult situations. Life often presents challenges and unexpected changes. When a person has a clear vision, they can adjust their plans without losing their overall direction. Instead of feeling lost, they continue moving forward with confidence because they know what they are working toward.

In the long run, vision acts like a guiding compass for life decisions. It helps people choose the right path, focus on meaningful opportunities, and stay committed to their personal growth. When individuals develop a clear vision for their future, their decisions become more thoughtful, purposeful, and aligned with the life they truly want to create.

Why Successful People Always Start with a Clear Vision

Successful people often begin their journey with a clear vision because it helps them understand what they truly want to achieve in life. A clear vision gives direction to their efforts and helps them focus on meaningful goals. Instead of working without purpose, they know where they want to go and what kind of future they want to build. This clarity allows them to plan their actions carefully and move forward with confidence.

A clear vision also helps successful people stay focused on long-term success rather than short-term comfort. Many people get distracted by temporary opportunities or easy choices that do not help them grow. However, when someone has a strong vision, they think carefully before making decisions. They choose actions that support their long-term goals instead of following what seems easy at the moment.

Vision also gives successful people a strong sense of motivation. When they clearly imagine the life they want to create, they feel inspired to work harder and learn new skills. Even when progress is slow, their vision reminds them why their effort is important. This motivation helps them stay committed to their journey.

Another reason successful people start with vision is that it helps them organize their goals and priorities. Life offers many possibilities, but without clear direction it is easy to become confused. Vision helps people decide what is truly important and what can be ignored. This ability to focus on priorities allows them to use their time and energy more effectively.

Vision also helps successful people remain strong during difficult situations. Every journey toward success includes challenges and failures. When people face obstacles, a clear vision reminds them of their purpose and keeps them moving forward. Instead of giving up, they learn from problems and continue improving themselves.

Over time, this clear sense of direction helps successful people build steady progress in their lives. Their vision guides their learning, their work, and their decisions. Because of this, they are able to create opportunities, develop strong skills, and move closer to their goals step by step. Vision becomes the foundation that supports their long-term success.

The Role of Imagination in Building Future Possibilities

When Ryan was young, he often spent time imagining the kind of life he wanted to live in the future. While many people around him only focused on their daily routine, Ryan liked to think about new ideas, better opportunities, and the possibilities that could exist beyond his current situation. His imagination allowed him to see a future that was different from his present life. It helped him believe that growth and improvement were possible if he was willing to learn and work for it.

Imagination is a powerful ability of the human mind. It allows people to think beyond what they see today and picture what their life could become tomorrow. When someone imagines a better future, their mind begins to search for ways to achieve it. This simple mental process often becomes the starting point of real progress. Many inventions, businesses, and creative ideas in the world began first as a simple thought in someone's imagination.

Ryan used his imagination not just to dream, but to guide his learning. Whenever he imagined the kind of person he wanted to become, he also started asking himself what skills and knowledge would help him reach that future. This thinking helped him choose what to study, how to spend his time, and which opportunities could help him grow. His imagination slowly turned into a practical guide for his decisions.

Imagination also helped Ryan stay hopeful during difficult times. There were moments when progress was slow and challenges appeared in his path. However, whenever he felt discouraged, he remembered the future he had once imagined. That picture of a better life gave him energy to continue moving forward and to keep improving himself step by step.

Many people underestimate the value of imagination because they think it is only related to creativity or childhood thinking. In reality, imagination is one of the first steps in building a meaningful future. When people allow themselves to imagine new possibilities, they expand their thinking and begin to see opportunities that others may ignore.

The story of Ryan shows that imagination can become a powerful tool for personal growth. It helps people move beyond their current limits and believe in new possibilities. When imagination is combined with learning, effort, and patience, it can slowly turn ideas into real achievements and open the door to a better future.

How Vision Creates Motivation and Direction

Vision gives a person a clear sense of purpose. When someone knows what they want to achieve in the future, their daily actions begin to feel more meaningful. Instead of working without a clear reason, they understand why their effort is important. This understanding naturally creates motivation from within. A clear vision helps people wake up each day with a stronger desire to move forward because they know their actions are connected to a bigger goal.

Motivation often becomes stronger when people can clearly imagine the results of their efforts. When a person has a vision of a better career, improved skills, or a more secure life, that image stays in their mind and encourages them to keep trying. Even when work feels difficult or progress is slow, the vision reminds them of the future they are working to build. This reminder keeps their energy and determination alive.

Vision also provides direction in life. Without direction, people may move from one activity to another without making real progress. They may spend time and effort on things that do not help them grow. A clear vision acts like a guiding path. It helps people understand which opportunities are valuable and which ones may lead them away from their goals.

Another important benefit of vision is that it improves decision making. When people face important choices, their vision helps them evaluate which option supports their future. Instead of feeling confused, they can choose actions that match their long-term purpose. This ability to make thoughtful decisions helps them move steadily toward their desired future.

Vision also encourages discipline and patience. Long-term success rarely happens quickly, and many goals require consistent effort over time. When people clearly understand what they are working toward, they become more willing to stay focused and continue learning. Their vision helps them remain committed even when challenges appear.

In the end, vision becomes both a source of motivation and a guide for direction. It gives people the reason to work harder and the clarity to choose the right path. When individuals develop a strong vision for their life, their efforts become more focused, their decisions become wiser, and their journey toward success becomes more meaningful.

Writing a Personal Vision Statement

A personal vision statement is a clear description of the life a person wants to create in the future. It helps people put their thoughts and dreams into simple words so they can understand their goals more clearly. When a person writes their vision, they begin to think seriously about their purpose, their values, and the direction they want their life to move. This process helps them become more aware of what truly matters to them.

Writing a personal vision statement also helps a person stay focused. Many people have good ideas about their future, but these ideas often remain only in their mind. When those ideas are written down, they become more real and meaningful. A written vision reminds a person of their goals and encourages them to stay committed to their path. It acts like a personal guide that helps them remember what they are working toward.

A strong vision statement should be simple, clear, and honest. It does not need complicated language or long explanations. The purpose of the vision statement is to express the kind of person someone wants to become and the kind of life they want to build. It may include goals related to career, learning, relationships, personal growth, and contribution to others.

Writing a vision statement also helps people make better decisions in daily life. When they face important choices, they can compare those choices with their vision. If an opportunity supports their long-term vision, it becomes easier to say yes. If it takes them away from their purpose, they can choose to avoid it. This clarity saves time and energy.

Another important benefit of writing a vision statement is that it increases motivation. When people read their own vision regularly, they remember why they started their journey. This reminder gives them strength during difficult times and encourages them to continue improving themselves.

Over time, a personal vision statement can also grow and change as a person learns more about life. It is not something that must remain exactly the same forever. Instead, it should reflect a person's learning, experiences, and evolving goals. By reviewing and improving their vision statement, people can keep their direction clear and continue moving toward a meaningful future.

Using Visualization Techniques for Goal Achievement

Sophia always had a goal of becoming a successful architect. She studied hard, but sometimes she felt tired and unsure about her progress. One day, her mentor suggested a simple practice—visualization. Every morning, Sophia started spending a few minutes imagining her future. She pictured herself designing buildings, working with a professional team, and seeing her ideas turn into real structures. This simple mental picture slowly changed the way she felt about her work. Her goal no longer seemed distant; it started to feel possible and real.

Visualization is a powerful mental technique where a person clearly imagines achieving their goals. Instead of only thinking about success in general words, the person creates a clear picture in their mind. They imagine the environment, the work they are doing, and the results they hope to achieve. This process helps the brain become more focused on the goal and encourages positive thinking.

When Sophia practiced visualization regularly, she noticed an important change in her mindset. She became more confident in her abilities because she could clearly imagine herself succeeding. This mental rehearsal prepared her mind for real situations. When challenges appeared in her studies or work, she felt more prepared to handle them because she had already imagined overcoming such situations.

Visualization also helps people stay motivated. Many goals require long periods of effort, and sometimes progress feels slow. When a person regularly imagines the successful result of their efforts, it reminds them why their work is important. This mental reminder creates emotional energy and encourages them to continue learning and improving.

Another benefit of visualization is that it helps people focus on opportunities that support their goals. When the mind becomes familiar with a clear image of success, it naturally begins to notice resources, ideas, and possibilities that may help achieve that goal. This increased awareness helps people make better decisions and use their time more wisely.

Over time, Sophia realized that visualization was not a replacement for hard work but a powerful tool that supported it. Her imagination gave her confidence, her learning built her skills, and her consistent effort slowly moved her closer to her dream. Visualization helped her believe in her future and strengthened her determination to make it real.

How Vision Helps Overcome Confusion and Uncertainty

Ethan was a young professional who often felt confused about his future. He worked hard every day, but he was not sure whether his efforts were leading him in the right direction. Sometimes he thought about changing his career, sometimes he considered starting a business, and other times he felt unsure about what skills he should learn. This constant uncertainty made him feel stressed and unmotivated because he did not know which path was truly right for him.

One evening, Ethan decided to take time to seriously think about his future instead of reacting to every new opportunity. He wrote down the kind of life he wanted to build in the next ten years. He thought about the type of work he enjoyed, the skills he wanted to master, and the lifestyle he hoped to create. As he reflected on these ideas, a clearer vision slowly started forming in his mind. For the first time, he felt that his future could have direction instead of confusion.

Once Ethan developed this vision, many of his daily decisions became easier. Earlier, he used to feel confused whenever a new opportunity appeared. Now he had a simple way to decide. If an opportunity helped him move closer to his long-term vision, he gave it his attention. If it did not match his direction, he politely moved away from it. This simple clarity removed much of the confusion he had experienced before.

Vision also helped Ethan stay calm during uncertain situations. In life, not everything goes according to plan. Sometimes projects fail, opportunities disappear, or unexpected challenges appear. Earlier, these situations made Ethan feel lost. But with a clear vision, he understood that temporary problems do not change the overall direction of his life. They only require adjustment and learning.

Over time, Ethan realized that confusion often comes from not knowing what we truly want. When people do not have a clear direction, every option looks equally important and decisions become difficult. Vision works like a compass that helps a person understand which direction to follow, even when the path is not completely clear.

Ethan's experience shows that vision does not remove every challenge, but it reduces uncertainty by giving life a clear purpose. When people know where they want to go, their thinking becomes calmer, their decisions become simpler, and their actions become more confident. A clear vision helps people move forward with courage even when the future is not fully predictable.

Keeping Your Vision Alive During Difficult Times

Lucas had a clear goal of building a successful career in technology. In the beginning, he was excited and full of energy. He studied new skills, worked on projects, and believed that his future would improve with time. But after a few years, things did not go as smoothly as he expected. Some opportunities did not work out, a few projects failed, and he started feeling tired and discouraged. During those moments, it became difficult for him to stay confident about his future.

Many people face similar situations when they are working toward their goals. The journey toward success is rarely simple or easy. Challenges, delays, and failures are normal parts of growth. During these times, a person may start doubting their abilities or questioning their direction. This is the moment when keeping a strong vision becomes very important. Vision reminds people why they started their journey in the first place.

Lucas decided not to give up on his long-term goal. Instead of focusing only on his current problems, he reminded himself of the future he wanted to create. He reviewed the vision he had written for himself and thought about the progress he had already made. This helped him see that temporary setbacks were only small parts of a much larger journey.

Keeping a vision alive during difficult times also requires patience and emotional strength. People need to accept that progress sometimes moves slowly. Learning new skills, building experience, and creating opportunities often take many years.

When a person remembers their vision during hard times, it helps them stay calm and continue working with determination.

Another helpful practice is surrounding oneself with positive influences such as books, mentors, and supportive people. These influences remind a person that challenges are normal and that many successful individuals also faced difficulties before reaching their goals. This understanding helps protect the vision from fading during stressful moments.

Over time, Lucas realized that difficult periods were not signs of failure but opportunities for learning and growth. Each challenge taught him new lessons and helped him become stronger and wiser. By holding onto his vision, he was able to continue moving forward step by step. His experience showed that vision is not only important during good times; it becomes even more powerful during moments of struggle.

Turning Vision into Daily Inspiration and Action

A clear vision becomes powerful only when it influences daily behavior. Many people have ideas about the future they want, but those ideas often remain only as thoughts. Vision begins to create real change when a person connects it with daily actions. When individuals clearly understand their long-term purpose, they start looking at their everyday activities differently. Simple tasks are no longer seen as small or unimportant; they become steps that slowly build the future they desire.

One important way to turn vision into daily inspiration is by reminding oneself of it regularly. When people keep their vision in their mind, it helps them stay focused on what truly matters. This reminder can come from writing goals, reviewing plans, or reflecting on long-term purpose. When the mind stays connected with a clear direction, motivation naturally grows because every action feels meaningful.

Vision also helps people create better daily habits. Instead of acting randomly, individuals begin to organize their time around activities that support their goals. Learning new skills, improving knowledge, and using time wisely become part of their routine. These small and consistent actions may seem simple at first, but over time they create strong progress and personal growth.

Another important benefit of turning vision into action is that it builds discipline. Long-term success rarely comes from sudden effort. It is usually the result of small actions repeated every day with patience. When people clearly understand their vision, they become more willing to stay consistent even when results take time. Their purpose gives strength to their efforts.

Vision also helps people stay positive and motivated during challenging situations. When progress feels slow or obstacles appear, remembering the larger goal helps maintain focus. Instead of losing energy or direction, individuals continue working because they understand that each small step contributes to their long-term success.

Over time, daily action guided by vision creates steady improvement in life. Skills grow stronger, decisions become wiser, and confidence increases. Vision acts as the guiding idea, while daily action turns that idea into real achievement. When people connect their vision with consistent effort, they begin to build the life they once imagined step by step.

2.

Turning Dreams into Goals

Understanding Why Dreams Need Structure

Dreams give hope and direction in life, but dreams alone are not enough to create success. Many people imagine a better future, but without a clear plan those dreams stay only in their mind. This is why dreams need structure. Structure means creating a simple plan, setting clear goals, and deciding the steps needed to move forward. When a dream has structure, it becomes easier to understand what needs to be done to achieve it.

Structure helps people turn big dreams into small and practical goals. A large dream can sometimes feel difficult or confusing, but when it is divided into smaller steps, it becomes easier to start working on it. These small steps help people stay focused and prevent them from feeling overwhelmed. Slowly, step by step, the dream begins to move closer to reality.

Another benefit of structure is that it helps people manage their time better. When someone has a clear plan, they know where to spend their energy and attention. Without structure, people may work hard but not see progress because their efforts are not organized. A simple structure helps guide daily actions in the right direction.

Structure also builds discipline and consistency. Success usually comes from regular effort, not from one big action. When people follow a plan and work on their goals every day, even small efforts start creating real progress over time. This steady effort slowly turns dreams into real achievements.

Structure also protects dreams from distractions. Life is full of activities and responsibilities that can easily take away attention. When people have a clear structure, they are more likely to stay focused on what truly matters and avoid wasting time on things that do not help their goals.

In the end, dreams supported by structure become stronger and more achievable. A dream gives the vision, but structure shows the path. When both work together, people can move forward with confidence and slowly build the life they truly want.

The Difference Between Dreams, Wishes, and Goals

In life, many people use the words dreams, wishes, and goals as if they mean the same thing, but they are actually different. Understanding this difference helps a person think more clearly about the future. A dream is a picture of the life someone wants to create. It is a big idea about success, happiness, growth, or achievement. Dreams give direction and inspiration because they help people imagine a better future for themselves.

A wish is different from a dream. A wish is usually a desire for something to happen without a clear plan or effort. People may wish for success, money, or opportunities, but wishing alone does not create results. Wishes depend mostly on luck or outside situations. Because of this, wishes often stay only as hopes rather than becoming real achievements.

A goal, however, is much more practical and powerful. A goal is when a person decides clearly what they want to achieve and begins to take action toward it. Goals include planning, effort, and commitment. When someone turns a dream into a goal, they start creating steps and actions that move them closer to their desired future.

Dreams give vision, wishes express desire, but goals create progress. This is why successful people focus more on goals than on wishes. They understand that dreams are important for motivation, but those dreams must be converted into clear and achievable targets.

When people learn to change their dreams into goals, their thinking becomes more focused. They begin to organize their time, improve their skills, and work with greater discipline. Slowly, the distance between imagination and reality becomes smaller.

In this way, understanding the difference between dreams, wishes, and goals helps individuals take more control of their future. Dreams inspire the mind, wishes express hope, but goals guide action. When a person focuses on clear goals, dreams stop being only ideas and start becoming real achievements.

The Importance of Clear and Measurable Goals

Clear and measurable goals help people move forward in life with focus and confidence. Many individuals have dreams about success, career growth, or financial stability, but without clear goals these dreams often remain only ideas. When a goal is clearly defined, a person understands exactly what they want to achieve. Measurable goals also allow people to track their progress and understand whether they are improving or not. This clarity helps reduce confusion and makes daily effort more meaningful.

Jack was a young professional who wanted to improve his career and build a better future. In the beginning, he often thought about becoming successful, but he did not know what actions would help him reach that point. His idea of success was too general, so he found himself working hard without seeing real progress. After some time, Jack realized that he needed clear and measurable goals instead of only having big dreams.

He decided to create simple and practical goals for himself. Instead of saying, "I want to become successful," Jack set a clear target to improve his professional skills within one year. He planned to complete several skill courses, read professional books, and practice new abilities every week. Because his goals were measurable, he could track how much he was learning and how much progress he was making each month.

This change in thinking helped Jack become more disciplined with his time. He started organizing his daily routine and focused more on activities that helped him grow. Each small improvement gave him motivation to continue working toward his larger goal. Over time, his skills improved and people around him started noticing his dedication and progress.

Clear and measurable goals also helped Jack stay focused during difficult moments. When work felt challenging or progress seemed slow, he would look at the goals he had set for himself. These goals reminded him why he started and encouraged him to continue moving forward with patience and effort.

In the end, Jack's journey shows an important lesson. Dreams become powerful when they are supported by clear and measurable goals. When people know exactly what they want to achieve and how they will measure their progress, their actions become more focused and consistent. Step by step, these clear goals help turn effort into real success.

Breaking Large Dreams into Smaller Goals

Large dreams often inspire people, but sometimes they can also feel difficult or far away. When a dream looks too big, many people feel confused about where to begin. This is why breaking large dreams into smaller goals is very important. Smaller goals make a big dream easier to understand and easier to achieve. Instead of thinking about the entire journey at once, a person can focus on one step at a time. This approach makes progress more practical and less stressful.

When a big dream is divided into smaller parts, it becomes clearer what actions need to be taken. For example, if someone dreams of building a successful career, the first steps may include learning new skills, gaining experience, and improving knowledge. Each of these steps becomes a small goal that can be completed with regular effort. Slowly, these smaller goals begin to build the path toward the larger dream.

Another advantage of smaller goals is that they help people stay motivated. When a person completes a small goal, it creates a feeling of progress and achievement. This positive feeling encourages them to continue working. Without these small milestones, the dream may feel too distant, and people may lose motivation before reaching their destination.

Breaking dreams into smaller goals also improves focus. Instead of worrying about the final result, individuals can concentrate on the task they need to complete today. This keeps the mind calm and helps people give their best effort to the present moment. Over time, these small efforts create steady improvement.

Smaller goals also help people manage time and energy better. When tasks are clear and manageable, it becomes easier to plan daily activities and avoid unnecessary distractions. Each completed step brings the person closer to the larger dream.

In the end, every great achievement is built through many small steps. Large dreams provide inspiration, but smaller goals create real progress. When people learn to divide their dreams into clear and achievable goals, they make the journey toward success more organized, focused, and achievable.

Setting Realistic and Achievable Targets

Setting realistic and achievable targets is an important step for personal growth and success. Many people create goals with strong excitement, but sometimes those goals are too difficult or unclear. When targets are not realistic, people may feel discouraged after some time because progress becomes hard to see. Realistic targets help individuals stay motivated because they create a clear path that can be followed with steady effort and patience.

A realistic target means setting a goal that matches a person's current abilities, time, and resources. It does not mean thinking small; instead, it means planning wisely. When people understand their starting point and create practical steps, they build a stronger foundation for progress. This thoughtful approach helps avoid frustration and allows improvement to happen gradually.

Achievable targets also help people build confidence. When a person completes a goal that was carefully planned, it creates a sense of success and satisfaction. This positive feeling encourages them to continue working toward the next target. Over time, many small achievements combine to create significant progress in life and career.

Another advantage of realistic targets is that they help people stay disciplined. When goals are clear and possible to achieve, individuals can organize their daily efforts more effectively. They learn to manage their time, focus on important activities, and avoid wasting energy on tasks that do not support their growth.

Realistic targets also allow room for learning and improvement. As people work toward their goals, they gain experience and discover new opportunities. This knowledge helps them adjust their plans and set better targets in the future. In this way, progress becomes continuous and sustainable.

In the long run, success is not created by sudden effort but by consistent actions guided by practical goals. When individuals set realistic and achievable targets, they move forward step by step with confidence. This balanced approach helps them transform their ambitions into steady and meaningful achievements.

The Importance of Deadlines in Goal Setting

Deadlines play an important role in turning goals into real results. Many people set goals with good intentions, but without a deadline those goals often get delayed or forgotten. A deadline creates a sense of urgency and reminds a person that time is limited. When people know they have a specific time to complete a task, they become more serious and focused about taking action.

Deadlines help people manage their time in a better way. Instead of working without direction, individuals begin to plan their activities according to the time available. They start giving priority to the most important tasks that move them closer to their goals. This helps them avoid wasting time and encourages them to stay productive throughout the day.

Another benefit of deadlines is that they improve discipline and commitment. When a person decides to complete a goal within a certain period, it creates responsibility. This responsibility motivates them to stay consistent with their efforts even when they feel distracted or tired. Over time, this discipline becomes a strong habit that supports long-term success.

Deadlines also make it easier to measure progress. When a goal has a time limit, people can check whether they are moving forward at the right speed. If progress is slow, they can adjust their efforts and improve their approach. This regular review helps individuals stay on the right path and prevents them from falling too far behind.

In addition, deadlines reduce the habit of procrastination. Without a time limit, people often delay important work because they feel there is always more time. A clear deadline removes this mindset and encourages immediate action. It pushes people to start working instead of waiting for the perfect moment.

In the end, deadlines give structure and direction to goals. They transform ideas into commitments and help people stay focused on completing what they started. When goals are supported by clear deadlines, individuals become more organized, disciplined, and productive, making it easier to achieve meaningful results in life.

Creating Short-Term and Long-Term Goals

Creating short-term and long-term goals helps a person move forward in life with clarity and purpose. Long-term goals represent the bigger vision a person wants to achieve in the future, such as building a successful career, starting a business, or achieving financial independence. These goals usually take many years of effort and learning. Short-term goals, on the other hand, are smaller and more immediate steps that help a person move toward that bigger vision. When both types of goals are planned together, they create a clear path that makes success more achievable.

Consider the example of two individuals, Luice and Hunt, who both wanted to improve their professional lives. Luice had a strong dream of becoming successful in his field, but he mostly focused on the final result. He often thought about the future he wanted, yet he did not create smaller goals to guide his daily actions. Because of this, he sometimes felt uncertain about what he should do next, and his progress became slow and inconsistent.

Hunt, however, decided to approach his future in a more structured way. He also had a long-term vision of building a strong and respected career, but he supported this vision with short-term goals. He planned to learn new skills every few months, complete professional courses, and improve his knowledge step by step. These short-term targets gave him a clear direction and helped him stay focused on daily improvement.

As time passed, Hunt began to notice steady progress. Each small goal he completed increased his confidence and helped him move closer to his larger ambition. Meanwhile, Luice still had the same dream, but without smaller steps he often felt stuck and unsure about how to move forward effectively.

This example shows the importance of balancing short-term and long-term goals. Long-term goals give people a clear vision of the future, while short-term goals provide the actions needed to reach that vision. When people break their big ambitions into smaller and manageable steps, they make the journey more practical and motivating.

In the end, success is built through consistent progress. Short-term goals act like steps on a staircase, while long-term goals represent the destination at the top. When individuals connect both together, they create a powerful system that helps them grow steadily and achieve meaningful success in life.

Aligning Goals with Personal Values

Setting goals is important for success, but those goals become more meaningful when they are connected with a person's personal values. Personal values are the beliefs and principles that guide how a person wants to live their life. These values may include honesty, growth, family, learning, helping others, or creating something meaningful. When goals are aligned with these values, people feel a deeper sense of purpose and satisfaction while working toward them.

Many individuals set goals based only on external influence such as social pressure, trends, or comparison with others. While such goals may look attractive from the outside, they often fail to bring long-term happiness because they are not connected with the person's true beliefs. When goals do not match personal values, people may lose motivation or feel empty even after achieving success.

Aligning goals with personal values helps people make better decisions in life. When individuals clearly understand what truly matters to them, they can choose goals that support their character and long-term vision. This clarity reduces confusion and helps them stay focused on paths that truly improve their life.

Another advantage of value-based goals is that they build stronger commitment. When a goal represents something meaningful, people are more willing to work hard and stay patient during challenges. Their effort feels purposeful because they know they are working toward something that truly matters to them.

This alignment also creates balance in life. For example, if a person values family, learning, and personal growth, they can design goals that support both career progress and personal well-being. This balanced approach helps individuals grow without sacrificing the things that give their life meaning.

In the long run, success becomes more fulfilling when it is guided by personal values. Goals provide direction, but values provide purpose. When both work together, people build a life that is not only successful on the outside but also meaningful and satisfying on the inside.

Writing Goals to Increase Commitment

Writing goals is a simple but powerful habit that increases a person's commitment toward success. Many people think about their goals in their mind, but when goals are only thoughts, they can easily be forgotten or ignored. Writing goals on paper or in a notebook makes them more real and clear. It helps the mind treat those goals as important responsibilities instead of temporary ideas.

When a person writes their goals, it brings clarity to their thinking. They begin to understand exactly what they want to achieve and why it matters to them. This process forces the mind to think carefully about the future. Instead of having vague ideas, written goals become clear statements that guide daily actions and decisions.

Writing goals also strengthens commitment because it creates a sense of personal responsibility. When people see their goals written in front of them, they are reminded of the promises they made to themselves. This reminder encourages them to stay focused and continue working even when motivation becomes low or challenges appear.

Another important benefit is that written goals help people organize their efforts. When goals are clearly written, it becomes easier to break them into smaller tasks and plan the steps needed to achieve them. This planning reduces confusion and helps individuals use their time and energy more effectively.

Written goals also allow people to track their progress. As individuals move forward, they can review their goals and see how much they have achieved. This progress builds confidence and encourages them to stay consistent with their efforts. It also helps them adjust their plans if necessary.

In the end, writing goals transforms ideas into commitments. A goal written with clear intention becomes a powerful reminder of a person's direction and purpose. When individuals regularly review and work toward their written goals, they develop stronger discipline, clearer focus, and a greater chance of turning their ambitions into real achievements.

Tracking Progress Regularly

Tracking progress regularly is an important habit for anyone who wants to achieve meaningful goals. Many people start working toward their goals with strong motivation, but they often forget to check how much progress they are actually making. When progress is not reviewed, it becomes difficult to understand whether the effort is moving in the right direction. Regular tracking helps people stay aware of their growth and keeps their focus strong.

When individuals track their progress, they begin to see the results of their daily efforts. Even small improvements become visible when they are recorded and reviewed. This creates a sense of achievement and encourages people to continue working with confidence. Seeing progress reminds them that consistent effort is slowly bringing them closer to their goals.

Another important benefit of tracking progress is that it helps identify mistakes and areas that need improvement. Sometimes people work hard but may follow an approach that is not effective. By reviewing their progress regularly, they can notice these issues early and make better decisions to improve their strategy. This learning process helps them grow faster and avoid repeating the same mistakes.

Tracking progress also strengthens discipline and accountability. When individuals know that they will review their work regularly, they become more responsible about completing their tasks. It encourages them to stay committed and use their time more wisely. This habit gradually builds a strong mindset focused on improvement and consistency.

Regular progress tracking also helps maintain motivation during slow periods. Sometimes results may take time to appear, but reviewing earlier improvements reminds people that growth is happening step by step. This awareness prevents discouragement and keeps their energy focused on long-term success.

In the end, success is not only about setting goals but also about observing the journey toward them. Tracking progress regularly allows people to stay aware, learn from their efforts, and adjust their actions when needed. This simple habit turns effort into continuous improvement and helps individuals move steadily toward their desired achievements.

Adjusting Goals When Necessary

Setting goals is important for progress, but it is equally important to adjust those goals when necessary. Life does not always move exactly as planned. New opportunities, challenges, and experiences can change a person's situation. When people remain flexible and willing to adjust their goals, they can continue moving forward instead of feeling stuck or discouraged. Adjusting goals is not a sign of failure; it is a sign of learning and growth.

As people work toward their goals, they gain new knowledge and better understanding of their abilities and environment. Sometimes a goal may turn out to be too difficult within the planned time, or sometimes it may become easier than expected. In such situations, adjusting the goal helps maintain balance. A goal can be modified by changing the timeline, improving the strategy, or breaking it into smaller steps.

This process also helps people stay realistic and practical in their approach. When individuals review their progress and make necessary changes, they prevent frustration and maintain steady motivation. Instead of feeling disappointed, they learn to improve their plan and continue moving in the right direction.

Adjusting goals also encourages continuous improvement. As people grow and gain experience, their vision often becomes clearer and stronger. They may discover better opportunities or develop new interests that align more closely with their long-term purpose. Updating goals allows them to take advantage of these positive changes.

Another important benefit is that it helps people stay focused on meaningful results rather than only following a fixed plan. A flexible mindset allows individuals to adapt to changing situations while still staying committed to their overall vision. This approach creates resilience and confidence during uncertain times.

In the end, successful people understand that goals are not rigid rules but guiding tools for progress. By reviewing and adjusting goals when necessary, individuals remain adaptable, focused, and motivated. This balanced approach helps them continue growing and steadily move toward a fulfilling and successful life.

Staying Motivated While Working Toward Goals

Staying motivated while working toward goals is very important for long-term success. In the beginning, people often feel excited and energetic about their goals, but after some time the journey can become challenging. Progress may feel slow, and daily responsibilities can reduce enthusiasm. During such moments, motivation helps a person continue moving forward instead of giving up. Understanding the purpose behind a goal can help maintain this motivation.

One effective way to stay motivated is by reminding oneself why the goal was set in the first place. When people remember the reason behind their efforts, their work begins to feel more meaningful. This connection between purpose and action helps individuals remain focused even when the process becomes difficult or tiring.

Another helpful method is to celebrate small progress. Large goals take time to achieve, but small achievements happen along the way. Recognizing these small improvements gives a sense of accomplishment and encourages a person to continue working. This positive reinforcement builds confidence and keeps motivation alive.

Maintaining a positive mindset also plays an important role in motivation. Challenges and obstacles are natural parts of any journey. When individuals see these difficulties as learning experiences rather than failures, they develop resilience. This mindset helps them stay strong and committed to their path.

Good habits and a disciplined routine also support motivation. When people create a regular schedule for working toward their goals, effort becomes a natural part of their daily life. Consistency reduces the need for constant motivation because the habit itself encourages action.

In the end, motivation is strengthened by purpose, progress, and persistence. When individuals stay connected to their goals, appreciate their small achievements, and maintain a positive attitude, they develop the inner strength needed to continue their journey. Step by step, this steady motivation leads them closer to achieving their dreams.

Celebrating Achievements Along the Journey

Celebrating achievements along the journey is an important part of personal growth and success. Many people focus only on the final result and forget to appreciate the progress they make along the way. However, every small achievement is a sign that effort is working and improvement is happening. When people recognize these moments, it creates happiness and motivation to continue moving forward.

Small achievements may include completing a difficult task, learning a new skill, improving a habit, or reaching a short-term goal. These moments may seem simple, but they show that a person is growing step by step. When individuals celebrate such progress, they build confidence in their abilities and feel encouraged to keep working toward their bigger goals.

Celebrating progress also helps reduce stress and pressure. The journey toward success can sometimes feel long and challenging. When people take time to appreciate their efforts and achievements, they develop a more positive mindset. This positive feeling helps them stay motivated even during difficult periods.

Another benefit of celebrating achievements is that it strengthens self-belief. When individuals look back and see how much they have already accomplished, they begin to trust their own ability to overcome challenges. This belief becomes a powerful source of strength for future goals.

Celebration does not always mean something big or expensive. It can be a simple moment of appreciation, sharing success with supportive people, or taking time to reflect on progress. These small actions remind a person that their effort is valuable and meaningful.

In the end, success is not only about reaching the final destination but also about appreciating the journey. When people celebrate their achievements along the way, they create a positive cycle of motivation, confidence, and growth that helps them continue moving toward their dreams with energy and enthusiasm.

3.

The Success Mindset

Understanding the Power of Mindset in Life Outcomes

Mindset is the way a person thinks about life, challenges, and opportunities. It strongly influences the results people create in their personal and professional lives. When individuals believe that they can learn, improve, and grow through effort, they develop a growth mindset. This type of thinking helps them stay positive and continue trying even when situations become difficult. A strong mindset allows people to see challenges as learning experiences rather than as permanent failures.

Consider the example of two individuals, Lucas and Kevin, who both started working in a new company. In the beginning, both of them faced pressure because the work required new skills and responsibilities. Lucas believed that every challenge was an opportunity to improve himself. Whenever he faced a difficult task, he stayed patient, asked questions, and spent extra time learning how to do the work better. His mindset helped him remain focused on growth instead of worrying about mistakes.

Kevin, however, reacted differently to the same situation. Whenever he faced a problem, he started thinking that the work was too difficult for him. Instead of trying to learn new methods, he often avoided challenging tasks. His negative thinking slowly reduced his confidence and stopped him from improving his abilities.

After some time, the difference between their mindsets became clear. Lucas kept improving because he believed in learning through effort and practice. His confidence and skills gradually increased, and he began receiving better opportunities at work. Kevin, on the other hand, remained at the same level because his thinking prevented him from taking initiative and learning new things.

This example shows that mindset plays a powerful role in shaping life outcomes. Two people may start with the same opportunities, but their thinking determines how they respond to challenges and how much they grow. A positive mindset encourages effort, learning, and persistence.

In the end, success in life is influenced not only by talent or circumstances but also by the way a person thinks. When individuals develop a strong and positive mindset, they become more capable of facing challenges, improving their abilities, and creating better results for their future.

Fixed Mindset vs Growth Mindset

The way a person thinks about their abilities and challenges is known as mindset. In life, people generally develop two types of thinking: a fixed mindset and a growth mindset. A fixed mindset is when a person believes that their abilities, intelligence, or talent cannot change. People with this mindset often think that they are either naturally good at something or not good at it at all. Because of this belief, they may avoid challenges, fear mistakes, and give up easily when they face difficulties.

On the other hand, a growth mindset is the belief that abilities can improve through learning, practice, and effort. People with this mindset understand that skills are not fixed and that improvement is always possible. Instead of fearing challenges, they see them as opportunities to learn and become better. They are more willing to try new things, accept feedback, and continue working even when progress is slow.

The difference between these two mindsets can strongly influence a person's success and personal development. A fixed mindset can limit growth because it creates fear of failure and discourages learning. People may avoid situations where they might make mistakes, which prevents them from gaining new knowledge and experience.

In contrast, a growth mindset encourages continuous improvement. When people believe they can learn from effort and experience, they become more patient and resilient. Mistakes are seen as lessons rather than failures, and challenges become chances to develop stronger skills. This attitude helps individuals grow both personally and professionally.

Another important benefit of a growth mindset is that it builds confidence over time. As people practice and see their improvement, they start believing more in their ability to handle difficult situations. This confidence encourages them to take on bigger goals and responsibilities.

In the end, mindset shapes how people approach life. A fixed mindset focuses on limitations, while a growth mindset focuses on possibilities. When individuals choose to develop a growth mindset, they open the door to learning, improvement, and greater success in many areas of life.

Building Strong Belief in Personal Abilities

Building strong belief in personal abilities is an important part of personal growth and success. When a person believes in their own potential, they become more confident in facing challenges and taking new opportunities. This belief helps individuals trust their skills and encourages them to try even when situations seem difficult. Without self-belief, people often doubt themselves and hesitate to take important steps in life.

Strong belief in personal abilities usually develops through learning, practice, and experience. Every time a person completes a task, solves a problem, or learns something new, their confidence slowly increases. These small experiences show that improvement is possible and that effort can create better results. Over time, this understanding helps individuals trust their ability to handle future challenges.

Another important way to build self-belief is by focusing on progress instead of perfection. Many people lose confidence because they expect perfect results from the beginning. However, real growth happens through patience and continuous effort. When people accept mistakes as part of learning, they become more willing to try again and improve their skills.

Supportive thoughts also play an important role in building belief. When individuals speak positively to themselves and focus on their strengths, they create a mindset that encourages growth. This positive thinking helps them stay calm and determined even during difficult situations.

Strong belief in personal abilities also encourages people to take responsibility for their goals. When individuals trust their capabilities, they are more likely to take action and remain committed to their plans. This commitment helps them develop discipline and determination over time.

In the end, belief in oneself becomes a powerful force for progress. When people trust their abilities and continue learning from their experiences, they build confidence step by step. This strong inner belief helps them face challenges with courage and move steadily toward their goals and dreams.

Removing Limiting Beliefs That Stop Progress

Limiting beliefs are thoughts that make a person believe they cannot achieve something or improve their situation. These beliefs often develop from past experiences, fear of failure, or negative opinions from others. When people accept these thoughts as truth, they begin to doubt their abilities and stop trying new opportunities. Over time, these beliefs create mental barriers that prevent growth and progress in life.

Removing limiting beliefs begins with awareness. A person must first recognize the negative thoughts that appear in their mind, such as "I am not capable," "I cannot succeed," or "This is too difficult for me." Once these thoughts are noticed, individuals can start questioning whether they are truly true or simply assumptions created by fear or past mistakes.

Another helpful step is replacing negative beliefs with more supportive and realistic thinking. Instead of focusing on what cannot be done, people can remind themselves that skills and abilities improve through learning and effort. When individuals believe that improvement is possible, they become more willing to try again and take positive action.

Learning from past experiences also helps remove limiting beliefs. Every mistake or failure contains lessons that can guide future decisions. When people see challenges as opportunities to grow instead of reasons to stop, they develop stronger confidence and resilience.

Surrounding oneself with positive influences also supports this process. Encouraging people, helpful knowledge, and inspiring examples can help change negative thinking patterns. These influences remind individuals that progress is possible when effort and learning continue.

In the end, removing limiting beliefs allows people to unlock their true potential. When individuals replace doubt with belief and focus on growth, they become more confident in taking action. This shift in thinking helps them move forward with courage and create better opportunities for success in life.

Developing Confidence Through Consistent Action

Confidence does not appear suddenly; it grows slowly through consistent action and repeated effort. Many people wait to feel confident before they start something new, but in reality confidence develops after a person begins taking action. When individuals take small steps toward their goals regularly, they begin to understand their abilities and trust themselves more. This process helps build a strong sense of self-belief over time.

Consistent action means doing the right activities again and again with patience. Even small efforts, when repeated daily or regularly, create improvement. As people practice their skills, complete tasks, and face challenges, they gain experience. This experience becomes the foundation for real confidence because it shows that they are capable of learning and solving problems.

Another important part of building confidence is accepting mistakes as part of growth. When people take action, mistakes will naturally happen. Instead of feeling discouraged, individuals can use these experiences as learning opportunities. Each lesson helps them improve their approach and become stronger in their abilities.

Consistency also reduces fear and hesitation. When a person repeatedly works toward a goal, the task slowly becomes more familiar and comfortable. What once felt difficult begins to feel manageable. This change helps people believe more in their skills and encourages them to take on bigger challenges.

Over time, consistent action also creates visible progress. When individuals see that their efforts are producing results, their confidence naturally increases. They begin to trust their ability to handle new situations and move forward with greater determination.

In the end, confidence is built through action, not just positive thinking. When people stay consistent with their efforts and continue learning from their experiences, they develop strong belief in themselves. This confidence becomes a powerful support that helps them achieve their goals and grow in many areas of life.

Training the Brain to Think Positively

Training the brain to think positively is an important step for improving mindset and creating better life outcomes. The human brain naturally focuses on problems and negative situations, but with practice it can learn to think in a more positive and balanced way. Positive thinking does not mean ignoring challenges; it means choosing to focus on solutions, growth, and opportunities instead of only worrying about difficulties. This type of thinking helps people stay calm, confident, and motivated in different situations.

One simple way to train the brain for positive thinking is by becoming aware of negative thoughts. Many times people automatically think things like "I cannot do this" or "This will never work." When individuals notice these thoughts, they can slowly replace them with more helpful ideas such as "I will try my best" or "I can learn and improve." This small change in thinking gradually builds a stronger and more hopeful mindset.

Another helpful method is focusing on gratitude and positive experiences. When people regularly think about the good things in their life, even small ones, it helps the brain develop a habit of noticing positive moments. This practice improves emotional balance and helps individuals maintain a healthy outlook even during difficult times.

Positive thinking also grows through supportive habits such as learning new skills, reading helpful ideas, and spending time with encouraging people. These influences guide the mind toward constructive thoughts and reduce unnecessary negativity. Over time, the brain becomes more comfortable focusing on possibilities rather than limitations.

Consistency is important in this process. Just like learning any new skill, positive thinking becomes stronger with regular practice. Each time a person chooses hopeful and constructive thoughts, the brain strengthens that pattern of thinking.

In the end, training the brain to think positively helps people develop confidence, resilience, and inner strength. When individuals learn to guide their thoughts toward growth and solutions, they become better prepared to handle challenges and create a more meaningful and successful life.

The Importance of Persistence in Success

Persistence is one of the most important qualities that helps people achieve success in life. It means continuing to work toward a goal even when challenges, failures, or difficulties appear. Many people start their journey with excitement, but only those who stay persistent are able to reach meaningful results. Persistence teaches patience, builds strong character, and helps individuals continue learning until they find the right path.

A simple story that explains the power of persistence is the journey of a man named Li Park. Li Park was born in a poor family and had very limited resources in the beginning of his life. He worked small jobs and faced many financial problems. Many times he failed in his early attempts to improve his situation. However, instead of losing hope, he decided to keep working and learning from every experience.

Li Park slowly started developing new skills and saving small amounts of money from his work. Even when progress was slow, he remained patient and continued improving himself. His persistence helped him see opportunities that others often ignored. Step by step, he started a small business and kept working hard to grow it.

The journey was not easy for him. There were times when he faced losses and difficulties, but his determination helped him continue moving forward. Instead of giving up, he focused on learning from each challenge and improving his decisions. Over time, his consistent effort started bringing better results.

Years later, Li Park's life changed completely. His business became successful, and he was able to create financial stability for himself and his family. What once seemed impossible slowly became reality because he never stopped trying. His story shows that success is often the result of long-term persistence rather than quick luck.

This example teaches an important lesson: persistence is the strength that turns dreams into achievements. When people remain patient, continue learning, and keep working even during difficult times, they increase their chances of reaching their goals and creating a better future.

Learning from Mistakes and Failures

Mistakes and failures are a natural part of life and personal growth. Every person experiences situations where things do not go as planned. Instead of seeing these moments as the end of progress, they can be used as valuable learning opportunities. When people learn from their mistakes, they gain knowledge and experience that helps them make better decisions in the future. This process slowly improves their abilities and understanding.

Many successful individuals have faced failures before achieving their goals. The difference is that they did not stop after making mistakes. Instead, they carefully looked at what went wrong and tried to understand the reason behind the failure. This attitude helps people grow stronger because they learn how to avoid the same mistakes again.

Learning from mistakes also builds resilience and patience. When individuals accept that errors are part of learning, they become less afraid of trying new things. This courage allows them to explore opportunities and develop new skills. Over time, these experiences increase their confidence and help them handle challenges more effectively.

Another benefit of learning from failure is that it encourages self-improvement. When people reflect on their actions, they begin to see areas where they can improve their knowledge, planning, or effort. This awareness helps them create better strategies and achieve better results in the future.

Mistakes also teach humility and understanding. They remind people that growth takes time and that no one becomes perfect instantly. This mindset encourages continuous learning and keeps individuals open to new ideas and improvements.

In the end, mistakes and failures are not obstacles but important teachers in life. When people accept them with a learning attitude, they turn difficult experiences into valuable lessons. This approach helps individuals become wiser, stronger, and more prepared for future success.

Developing Patience for Long-Term Success

Patience is an important quality for achieving long-term success. Many people want quick results, but most meaningful achievements take time, effort, and continuous learning. When individuals understand that progress is a gradual process, they become more patient with their journey. Patience helps people stay calm and focused even when results are not immediate.

Long-term success often requires consistent effort over many months or even years. During this time, people may face challenges, slow progress, or temporary failures. Patience allows individuals to continue working without becoming discouraged. Instead of giving up, they learn to trust the process and remain committed to their goals.

Developing patience also helps people make better decisions. When someone acts with patience, they think carefully before taking action. This thoughtful approach reduces unnecessary mistakes and helps them choose the most effective path toward their goals. Patience encourages planning, discipline, and steady improvement.

Another benefit of patience is that it helps people handle pressure and difficulties in a balanced way. When individuals accept that success requires time, they stop comparing themselves with others and focus more on their own progress. This mindset creates a healthier and more positive attitude toward personal growth.

Patience also allows skills and knowledge to develop naturally. Just like learning a new language or mastering a profession, real expertise grows through regular practice and experience. When people remain patient, they give themselves the time needed to improve step by step.

In the end, patience becomes a powerful strength in the journey toward success. It helps individuals stay committed, make wise decisions, and continue improving even during slow periods. When people develop patience, they create a strong foundation that supports lasting growth and meaningful achievements in life.

Building Mental Discipline and Resilience

Mental discipline and resilience are important qualities for handling challenges and achieving success in life. Mental discipline means the ability to control thoughts, emotions, and actions so that a person can stay focused on their goals. Resilience means the strength to recover from difficulties and continue moving forward. When these two qualities develop together, they help individuals remain strong even during stressful or uncertain situations.

Building mental discipline begins with creating good habits and following them consistently. Simple actions such as managing time wisely, completing responsibilities, and staying focused on important tasks help strengthen the mind. When people practice discipline regularly, they train themselves to avoid distractions and remain committed to their goals. Over time, this consistency builds a strong sense of self-control.

Resilience develops when people learn how to face challenges without giving up. Difficult situations are part of every journey, but resilient individuals see them as opportunities to learn and grow. Instead of feeling defeated by problems, they look for solutions and continue improving their approach. This attitude helps them remain positive even when progress becomes difficult.

Another way to build these qualities is by maintaining a balanced mindset. When people learn to manage stress, stay calm during pressure, and focus on solutions, their mental strength increases. Positive thinking, self-reflection, and learning from experiences all contribute to stronger resilience.

Mental discipline and resilience also help people stay motivated for long-term goals. When individuals have control over their thoughts and emotions, they can continue working even when motivation becomes low. This inner strength keeps them moving forward with determination.

In the end, mental discipline and resilience create a strong foundation for personal and professional growth. These qualities help individuals remain focused, overcome difficulties, and continue learning from every experience. With a disciplined and resilient mind, people become better prepared to face challenges and achieve lasting success in life.

Surrounding Yourself with Positive Influences

Surrounding yourself with positive influences can strongly shape the direction of your life. Every person is affected by the people they spend time with, the ideas they listen to, and the environment they live in. When individuals stay close to people who encourage growth, learning, and responsible thinking, they naturally begin to develop similar habits. Positive influences guide the mind toward improvement and help a person focus on meaningful goals rather than temporary distractions.

Positive people usually share helpful advice, constructive feedback, and encouragement during difficult moments. Their words and actions remind others that challenges are part of growth and that progress comes from patience and effort. Being around such individuals helps people stay motivated and confident even when situations become challenging.

Another important benefit of positive influences is that they raise a person's standards. When individuals see others working hard, learning new skills, and staying disciplined, it encourages them to improve their own habits. This creates a healthy environment where people inspire each other to grow and achieve more. Over time, these small influences can change the way a person thinks and acts.

Positive influences also protect individuals from negative thinking and unproductive habits. When someone is surrounded by supportive and thoughtful people, they are less likely to fall into discouraging attitudes such as constant complaining, self-doubt, or lack of direction. Instead, they learn to focus on solutions, opportunities, and continuous self-improvement.

A valuable step in life is to choose carefully the people, information, and environments that shape daily thinking. Reading inspiring ideas, learning from experienced mentors, and spending time with people who believe in growth can create a strong foundation for personal development. These influences quietly guide decisions and help individuals remain focused on what truly matters.

In the long run, the company a person keeps becomes a powerful force in shaping their future. When individuals intentionally surround themselves with positive influences, they create an environment that encourages learning, discipline, and meaningful progress. This choice not only improves personal success but also builds a mindset that supports a balanced and purposeful life.

4.

Why Goals Fail

Lack of Clarity in Defining Goals

Lack of clarity in defining goals can create confusion in a person's life and stop them from making real progress. When people do not clearly decide what they want to achieve, their efforts become scattered. They may work hard every day, but without a clear direction their actions do not lead to strong results. Clear goals act like a guide that shows where a person should focus their time, energy, and learning. When the mind understands the destination, it becomes easier to stay disciplined and move forward with purpose.

When goals are unclear, people often follow temporary opportunities instead of a long-term plan. They may start one thing and quickly switch to another because they are not sure about their real purpose. This habit slowly reduces confidence and creates frustration. But when a person clearly defines their goals, they can build a strong plan and take consistent action every day. Clarity helps them understand which opportunities are useful and which ones should be avoided.

To understand this idea better, imagine two individuals named Denis and Lucifer. Denis has a clear goal for his future. He wants to develop valuable skills, build financial stability, and grow step by step in his career. Because his goals are clear, he plans his time carefully, learns new things regularly, and focuses on activities that help him grow. Even when challenges appear, Denis stays patient because he knows where he is going. His clear direction helps him make better decisions and slowly build a successful life.

On the other hand, Lucifer does not clearly define his goals. He says he wants success, but he never decides what success truly means for him. Sometimes he wants quick money, sometimes he changes his interests, and sometimes he simply follows what others are doing. Because his goals are not clear, his actions also become inconsistent. He works hard at times but loses focus easily, and his progress becomes slow and uncertain.

This comparison shows how clarity can shape a person's life path. Denis moves forward with purpose because he understands his goals, while Lucifer keeps changing direction because he lacks clarity. When people take time to define their goals clearly, they gain better control over their future and use their efforts in a more productive way. Clear goals create focus, confidence, and steady progress toward a better life.

Setting Unrealistic Expectations

Setting unrealistic expectations can create unnecessary pressure and disappointment in life. Many people expect quick success, fast results, or perfect outcomes without understanding that real progress takes time and consistent effort. When expectations are too high or unrealistic, even small delays or difficulties can make a person feel discouraged. Instead of appreciating gradual improvement, they start believing that they are failing, even when they are actually making progress.

Unrealistic expectations often come from comparing our journey with others. People see someone's success and assume that it happened quickly or easily. In reality, most achievements come after years of learning, practice, and patience. When individuals expect immediate results, they may lose motivation when things do not happen as fast as they imagined. This mindset can lead to frustration and sometimes even make people give up on their goals too early.

A better approach is to set realistic and achievable expectations. This means understanding that every goal requires time, learning, and effort. When people accept that progress happens step by step, they become more patient with their journey. Small improvements start to feel valuable because they are seen as part of a bigger process of growth.

Realistic expectations also help people stay mentally balanced. Instead of putting extreme pressure on themselves, they focus on consistent effort and steady learning. This creates a healthier mindset where progress is measured through improvement rather than perfection. Over time, this approach builds stronger confidence and resilience.

Another helpful practice is breaking large goals into smaller milestones. When a big goal is divided into smaller targets, it becomes easier to manage and track progress. Achieving these small milestones creates motivation and helps individuals stay committed to their long-term vision.

In the end, realistic expectations allow people to grow with patience and wisdom. When individuals understand that success is a gradual process, they stay focused on learning, improving, and moving forward steadily. This balanced mindset helps them build a stable path toward lasting achievement and personal growth.

Fear of Failure and Self-Doubt

Fear of failure and self-doubt are two common obstacles that stop many people from reaching their true potential. When individuals constantly worry about failing, they often avoid taking important opportunities in life. Instead of trying something new, they remain in their comfort zone because they are afraid of making mistakes or being judged by others. This fear slowly limits growth and prevents people from discovering their real abilities.

Self-doubt also affects the way people think about themselves. When a person repeatedly questions their skills and decisions, their confidence becomes weak. Even when they have the ability to succeed, negative thoughts make them believe that they are not capable enough. Over time, this mindset can stop them from taking action and achieving their goals.

However, failure is a natural part of learning and improvement. Every successful person has faced challenges, mistakes, and setbacks during their journey. Instead of seeing failure as something negative, it should be understood as an opportunity to learn valuable lessons. Each mistake teaches something important that helps a person grow stronger and wiser.

One helpful way to overcome fear and self-doubt is to focus on small actions instead of worrying about the final result. When people start with small steps, they slowly build confidence through experience. Each completed task creates a sense of progress and encourages them to continue moving forward.

Another useful habit is practicing positive self-talk. The way people speak to themselves has a strong impact on their mindset. Replacing negative thoughts with encouraging words can slowly change how a person sees their abilities. Believing in gradual improvement helps individuals develop stronger confidence over time.

In the end, fear of failure and self-doubt can only control life if a person allows them to. When individuals choose to face challenges with courage and learn from every experience, they begin to grow beyond their fears. This mindset helps them build confidence, develop resilience, and move closer to their personal and professional goals.

Lack of Proper Planning

Lack of proper planning is one of the major reasons why many people struggle to achieve their goals. When individuals start working without a clear plan, they may feel busy but their efforts do not always produce strong results. Planning helps a person organize their time, resources, and actions in the right direction. Without planning, people often face confusion, delays, and unnecessary mistakes that slow down their progress.

Proper planning helps individuals understand what steps are

required to reach a goal. When a person plans their actions carefully, they can identify the most important tasks and focus their energy on completing them. This makes work more organized and productive. On the other hand, when planning is ignored, people may jump from one task to another without completing anything properly.

Planning also helps in managing time effectively. Many people complain that they do not have enough time, but often the real problem is not time but poor planning. When tasks are scheduled in advance, it becomes easier to balance work, learning, and personal responsibilities. This structure reduces stress and helps individuals stay disciplined in their daily routine.

Another benefit of planning is that it prepares people for possible challenges. When individuals think about their actions in advance, they can also consider possible problems and prepare solutions. This makes them more confident and ready to handle unexpected situations without losing focus on their goals.

A simple way to develop better planning is by writing down daily or weekly priorities. When people clearly list the tasks that must be completed, their mind becomes more focused and organized. This habit helps them avoid distractions and stay committed to important activities that support their long-term growth.

In the end, proper planning acts like a strong foundation for success. It helps people use their time wisely, reduce confusion, and stay focused on their goals. When individuals learn to plan their actions carefully, they create a clear path that leads to steady improvement and better results in life.

Procrastination and Delaying Action

Procrastination means delaying important work even when a person knows that the task should be completed. Many people postpone their responsibilities by saying they will start later or tomorrow. This habit may feel comfortable in the short term, but over time it creates stress, pressure, and missed opportunities.

When action is delayed again and again, small tasks turn into big problems that become harder to manage.

One common reason for procrastination is feeling overwhelmed by a task. When a goal or responsibility looks too big, the mind tries to avoid it. Instead of starting the work, people distract themselves with less important activities such as using social media, watching videos, or doing unnecessary tasks. This gives temporary relief but does not solve the real problem.

Procrastination also reduces confidence and productivity. When people delay their work, they often feel guilty or disappointed in themselves. This negative feeling can reduce motivation and make it even harder to start the task later. Over time, this cycle of delay can stop a person from reaching their goals.

A simple way to overcome procrastination is to start with small and manageable steps. Instead of thinking about completing the whole task, individuals can focus on doing just the first step. Once they begin, the mind becomes more engaged and it becomes easier to continue working. Starting is often the hardest part, but it creates momentum for progress.

Another helpful habit is setting clear deadlines and creating a daily routine. When tasks have a specific time for completion, people become more disciplined about their responsibilities. A structured routine reduces distractions and helps individuals stay focused on important work.

In the end, taking timely action is one of the most powerful habits for personal growth. When people stop delaying their responsibilities and start acting on their goals, they build discipline, confidence, and productivity. Consistent action, even in small steps, can create strong progress and lead to a more successful and organized life.

Negative Influence from Environment

Negative influence from the environment can strongly affect a person's mindset, decisions, and overall direction in life. The environment includes the people we spend time with, the conversations we listen to, and the habits we observe around us. When someone is surrounded by negativity, constant criticism, or people who lack motivation, it becomes difficult to stay positive and focused on personal goals. Over time, this type of environment can slowly reduce confidence and limit a person's thinking.

Many individuals do not realize how much their surroundings shape their behavior. If the people around them often complain, avoid responsibility, or discourage new ideas, it can create a mindset where growth feels difficult. A person may start believing that success is not possible or that their efforts will not make a difference. This kind of influence can stop people from trying new opportunities or improving their skills.

On the other hand, a positive environment encourages learning, discipline, and progress. When individuals are surrounded by supportive and hardworking people, they feel inspired to improve themselves. Positive discussions, helpful advice, and shared goals can motivate a person to stay committed to their personal development.

To reduce negative influence, it is important to become aware of the environment around us. People should try to spend more time with individuals who encourage growth, learning, and responsible thinking. Reading good books, listening to educational content, and learning from positive role models can also help create a healthier mental environment.

Another important step is developing strong self-awareness. Even when negative influences are present, a person can choose how they respond to them. By focusing on personal values and long-term goals, individuals can protect their mindset from harmful opinions and distractions.

In the end, the environment we choose plays a powerful role in shaping our future. When people consciously surround themselves with positive influences and supportive ideas, they create a strong foundation for personal growth, better decisions, and a more successful life.

Lack of Consistency and Discipline

Lack of consistency and discipline is one of the biggest reasons why many people fail to achieve their goals. Many individuals start their work or personal goals with great excitement and motivation, but after some time they lose focus and stop putting in regular effort. Success in any area of life does not come from occasional effort; it comes from consistent actions repeated over a long period of time. Without discipline, it becomes easy to get distracted by comfort, entertainment, or temporary interests.

Consistency means doing the necessary work regularly, even on days when motivation is low. Many people depend only on motivation, but motivation does not stay the same every day. Discipline helps a person continue working even when they do not feel like it. This habit slowly builds strong character and teaches responsibility toward personal goals and commitments.

When consistency is missing, progress becomes slow and unstable. A person may work hard for a few days and then stop for many days. This pattern breaks the learning process and makes it harder to develop skills or complete important tasks. Over time, this can create frustration because the results do not match the effort that was initially started.

Developing discipline begins with small daily habits. Instead of trying to change everything at once, a person can start by committing to small actions every day. These small efforts may seem simple, but when repeated regularly they create powerful results over time. Discipline grows stronger when actions become part of a daily routine.

Another important step is reducing distractions and staying focused on priorities. When people clearly understand what is important in their life, it becomes easier to avoid activities that waste time and energy. Protecting time for learning, work, and self-improvement helps maintain consistency.

In the end, consistency and discipline are powerful qualities that shape a person's success. When individuals learn to show up every day and continue their efforts patiently, they slowly build progress, confidence, and strong habits that lead them toward a better and more successful future.

Ignoring Progress Tracking

Ignoring progress tracking is a common mistake that can slow down personal and professional growth. Many people work hard toward their goals, but they do not take time to check how much progress they have actually made. Without tracking progress, it becomes difficult to understand whether the efforts are moving in the right direction or if changes are needed. Progress tracking helps people stay aware of their improvement and keeps their goals clear in their mind.

When progress is not measured, a person may feel confused about their results. They might think they are not improving, even when small progress is happening. This can reduce motivation and make them feel discouraged. But when progress is tracked regularly, people can clearly see their improvement, which builds confidence and encourages them to continue their efforts.

Tracking progress also helps people identify mistakes and areas that need improvement. When individuals review their work, habits, or learning regularly, they can notice what is working well and what needs to be changed. This awareness allows them to adjust their actions and make better decisions for future growth.

A simple way to track progress is by writing down goals and reviewing them weekly or monthly. People can note the steps they completed, the skills they improved, and the challenges they faced. This process creates a clear record of their journey and helps them stay focused on their long-term goals.

Another benefit of progress tracking is that it builds discipline and accountability. When individuals know they will review their progress, they become more serious about completing their tasks. This habit encourages consistency and helps maintain focus on meaningful activities.

In the end, tracking progress is an important part of achieving any goal. It helps people stay aware of their growth, learn from their experiences, and make better decisions for the future. When individuals regularly measure their progress, they gain clarity, motivation, and a stronger sense of direction in their journey toward success.

Failing to Learn from Past Mistakes

Failing to learn from past mistakes can stop a person from growing and improving in life. Everyone makes mistakes, but the real value of a mistake comes from the lesson it teaches. When people ignore these lessons or refuse to reflect on their actions, they may repeat the same problems again and again. Instead of moving forward with better understanding, they remain stuck in the same patterns that slow down their progress.

Many individuals feel uncomfortable thinking about their mistakes because it reminds them of failure or disappointment. However, avoiding these experiences does not solve the problem. Mistakes are valuable teachers that show what went wrong and what can be improved. When people take time to understand their past decisions, they gain wisdom that helps them make better choices in the future.

Learning from mistakes also builds stronger awareness and responsibility. When a person honestly accepts their errors, they become more careful and thoughtful in their actions. This attitude helps them avoid repeating the same problems and encourages personal growth. Instead of blaming others or situations, they focus on improving their own thinking and behavior.

A useful habit is to reflect on past experiences regularly. People can ask themselves simple questions such as: What mistake did I make? What lesson did I learn from it? What can I do differently next time? These questions help turn a negative experience into a valuable learning opportunity.

Another important step is to stay patient with personal growth. Improvement does not happen instantly. Learning from mistakes takes time, awareness, and honest self-reflection. When individuals accept this process, they become more resilient and better prepared to face future challenges.

In the end, mistakes are not the real problem; ignoring the lessons from them is. When people choose to learn from their past experiences, they gain knowledge, maturity, and stronger decision-making skills. This mindset helps them grow wiser and move closer to a more successful and responsible life.

5.

Your Life Blueprint

Understanding the Importance of Life Planning

Understanding the importance of life planning helps a person create a clear direction for their future. Life planning means thinking carefully about what we want to achieve and how we will reach those goals over time. Many people move through life without a clear plan, simply reacting to situations as they come. While this may work for a short time, it often leads to confusion and missed opportunities. A clear life plan helps individuals focus their energy on actions that support their long-term growth and stability.

Life planning also helps people make better decisions. When a person has a clear vision for their future, it becomes easier to choose activities, habits, and opportunities that support that vision. Without planning, people may spend time on things that do not contribute to their progress. Planning acts like a guide that keeps individuals moving in the right direction and helps them avoid unnecessary distractions.

Another important benefit of life planning is that it builds confidence and discipline. When people know what they want to achieve, they become more serious about their daily actions. They start managing their time better, learning useful skills, and focusing on activities that bring them closer to their goals. This structured approach creates stability and helps individuals feel more in control of their future.

To understand this idea clearly, imagine two individuals named Jackson and Nick. Jackson spends time thinking about his future and creates a simple life plan. He decides what skills he wants to develop, what career he wants to build, and how he will improve his life step by step. Because of this plan, Jackson uses his time wisely and stays focused on actions that support his long-term growth. Even when challenges appear, his plan helps him stay motivated and continue moving forward.

Nick, on the other hand, does not think much about planning his future. He mostly lives day by day and makes decisions based on temporary situations. Sometimes he works hard, but without a clear direction his efforts become scattered. Because he does not have a long-term plan, he often feels uncertain about his progress and future opportunities.

This simple comparison shows how life planning can shape a person's journey. Jackson moves forward with clarity and purpose because he planned his path, while Nick experiences confusion because he did not think about his future direction. When individuals understand the importance of life planning, they create a strong foundation that helps them build a stable, successful, and well-organized life.

Identifying Personal Values and Priorities

Identifying personal values and priorities helps a person understand what is truly important in life. Values are the things we believe in, like honesty, growth, respect, and hard work. When a person is clear about these values, they can take better decisions and stay focused on the right path. Without clear values, people often get distracted and follow others, which can lead to confusion and lack of satisfaction in life.

Knowing your priorities means deciding what deserves your time and energy the most. Life gives many options, but not everything is equally important. When you set clear priorities, you start focusing on things that bring real progress, like learning new skills, improving health, or building a strong career. This helps you avoid wasting time on activities that do not support your future.

Personal values also act like a guide in difficult situations. When you face confusion or pressure, your values help you stay strong and make the right choice. This builds self-respect and confidence because you know you are living according to your own principles, not just following others.

A simple way to identify your values is to ask yourself what truly matters to you and what kind of life you want to live. Think about the people you respect and the qualities they have. These reflections can help you understand your own beliefs and priorities more clearly.

When you live according to your values and focus on your priorities, your life becomes more organized and meaningful. You stop running behind everything and start moving in a clear direction. This clarity helps you grow faster and achieve better results with less confusion.

In the end, identifying personal values and priorities is not just about thinking, it is about applying them in daily life. Small decisions made with clarity and purpose can create a strong and successful future.

Understanding Strengths and Weaknesses

Understanding your strengths and weaknesses is very important for personal growth and success. Strengths are the skills and qualities you are naturally good at, while weaknesses are the areas where you need improvement. When a person clearly understands both, they can use their strengths in the best way and work on improving their weak areas step by step. Without this understanding, people may waste time on the wrong things and feel stuck in their progress.

Knowing your strengths helps you build confidence and perform better in life. When you focus on what you are good at, you can achieve results faster and feel more motivated. At the same time, accepting your weaknesses is equally important. It does not mean you are not capable, it simply shows where you need to learn and

improve. This balanced thinking helps you grow in a practical and realistic way.
Many people ignore their weaknesses or feel afraid to face them. But real growth starts when you accept your weak points and take small actions to improve them. For example, if communication is a weak area, you can practice speaking daily or learn from others. Small improvements over time can create big changes in your life.
Another important point is that you should not compare your strengths and weaknesses with others. Every person has a different journey. Instead of comparing, focus on self-improvement and becoming better than your past version. This mindset helps you stay positive and focused on growth.
A simple way to understand your strengths and weaknesses is by observing your daily activities. Notice where you perform well and where you struggle. You can also take feedback from trusted people who can guide you honestly. This helps you get a clear picture of yourself.
When you truly understand your strengths and weaknesses, you can make better decisions, choose the right opportunities, and grow with clarity. This awareness becomes a strong foundation for building a successful and balanced life.

Creating a Long-Term Life Vision

Creating a long-term life vision means having a clear picture of the kind of life you want to build in the future. It is not just about short-term goals, but about understanding where you want to reach in the next 5, 10, or even 20 years. When a person has a clear vision, their daily actions start moving in the right direction. Without a vision, people often feel confused and keep changing their path without real progress.
A long-term vision helps you stay focused and motivated. When you know what you are working for, it becomes easier to avoid distractions and stay committed to your goals. It gives a sense of purpose and direction, which is very important for long-term

success. Even during tough times, a clear vision reminds you why you started and helps you keep going.

Creating a life vision does not mean everything will go exactly as planned. Life can change, and situations may not always be in your control. But having a vision gives you a strong base to adjust your plans without losing direction. It helps you stay stable even when challenges come.

To create a strong life vision, start by asking yourself simple questions. What kind of life do you want? What type of work makes you happy? What kind of lifestyle do you want to live? These questions help you think deeply and create a clear image of your future.

Once your vision is clear, break it into smaller goals and actions. Big dreams can feel difficult, but when you divide them into small steps, they become easier to achieve. This process makes your vision practical and achievable over time.

In the end, a long-term life vision acts like a roadmap for your journey. It helps you stay focused, make better decisions, and move forward with confidence. When your vision is clear, your actions become powerful, and your chances of success increase in a strong and steady way.

Designing a Clear Life Direction

Designing a clear life direction means deciding where you want to go in life and how you will reach there step by step. Many people feel lost because they do not have a clear direction, so they keep changing their path and do not see real progress. When your direction is clear, your thoughts and actions become focused, and you start using your time in a better way.

A clear life direction helps you make better decisions. When opportunities come, you can easily decide whether they match your goals or not. This saves your time and energy and keeps you away from unnecessary distractions. Without direction, even hard work may not give good results because the effort is not focused.

To design your life direction, first understand what you truly want from life. Think about your interests, strengths, and the kind of lifestyle you want to build. This will help you choose a path that suits you. Once you are clear, set simple goals and create a plan to move forward step by step.

It is also important to stay flexible. Sometimes situations change, and you may need to adjust your direction slightly. This is normal. The goal is not to be perfect but to keep moving in the right direction with learning and improvement.

Another important point is consistency. A clear direction only works when you take regular action. Small daily steps, taken with focus, can create big results over time. Discipline and patience play a key role in staying on the right path.

In the end, designing a clear life direction gives you purpose, clarity, and confidence. It helps you move forward with a plan instead of confusion. When you know where you are going, every step becomes more meaningful, and your journey becomes more successful and fulfilling.

Building Personal and Professional Growth Plans

Building personal and professional growth plans means creating a clear path to improve yourself in both life and career. Personal growth focuses on habits, mindset, health, and self-discipline, while professional growth focuses on skills, knowledge, and career progress. When you plan both areas together, your overall life becomes more balanced and successful. Without a plan, growth becomes slow and directionless.

A clear growth plan helps you understand what you need to improve and how you will do it. It allows you to set simple and practical goals, like learning a new skill, improving communication, or becoming more disciplined in daily life. These small goals, when followed consistently, create strong long-term results.

It is important to focus on learning and skill development. In today's world, continuous learning is necessary for growth. When you improve your skills regularly, your value increases, and better opportunities start coming to you. This helps you grow professionally and build a stable career.

At the same time, personal growth should not be ignored. Qualities like patience, confidence, positive thinking, and time management are equally important. These qualities help you handle challenges, stay motivated, and perform better in both personal and professional life.

To build a strong growth plan, start by identifying your current position and your desired future. Then create a step-by-step plan with small daily or weekly actions. Track your progress and make improvements when needed. This keeps you focused and moving forward.

In the end, building personal and professional growth plans gives you clarity and control over your future. It helps you grow in a structured way, improve your abilities, and achieve success with confidence and consistency.

Setting Priorities for Success

Setting priorities for success means deciding what tasks and goals are most important and giving them your full attention. In daily life, there are many activities that can take your time, but not all of them help you move forward. When you do not set clear priorities, you may stay busy all day but still feel that you are not making real progress. Priorities help you focus on what truly matters and avoid wasting time on less important things.

When a person sets the right priorities, their work becomes more organized and effective. They start focusing on tasks that bring real results, such as learning new skills, completing important work, or improving their habits. This focused effort increases productivity and helps achieve goals faster. Without priorities, people often get distracted by small or easy tasks and ignore the important ones.

Setting priorities also helps reduce stress and confusion. When you know what needs to be done first, your mind becomes clear and calm. You do not feel overwhelmed because you are following a clear plan. This makes it easier to manage time and complete tasks in a disciplined way.

A simple method to set priorities is to list your daily or weekly tasks and identify which ones are most important for your growth. Start your day by completing these important tasks first. This habit ensures that your energy is used in the best way and your goals remain the main focus.

It is also important to learn to say no to distractions and unnecessary activities. Not every opportunity or request deserves your time. When you protect your time and stay focused on your priorities, you create better results and avoid unnecessary stress.

In the end, setting priorities is a powerful step toward success. It helps you use your time wisely, stay focused on your goals, and move forward with clarity. When you give importance to the right things, your efforts become more meaningful, and your chances of achieving success increase greatly.

Creating a Structured Life Roadmap

Creating a structured life roadmap means making a clear and organized plan for your future. It helps you understand where you are now, where you want to go, and how you will reach there step by step. Without a roadmap, people often feel confused and move in different directions without clear results. A structured plan gives direction and helps you use your time and energy in the right way.

A life roadmap divides big goals into smaller and practical steps. When goals are too large, they can feel difficult and overwhelming. But when you break them into simple actions, they become easier to manage and achieve. This step-by-step approach helps you stay focused and motivated throughout your journey.

Having a roadmap also improves decision making. When you have a clear plan, you can easily choose what actions support your goals and what actions should be avoided. This saves time and reduces distractions, allowing you to focus only on what truly matters for your growth.

A structured roadmap also helps in tracking progress. When you follow a plan, you can regularly check how much you have achieved and what still needs to be done. This creates awareness and helps you improve your actions when needed. It keeps you on the right path and prevents you from going off track.

To create a strong life roadmap, start by setting a clear long-term vision. Then break it into short-term goals and daily actions. Keep your plan simple and flexible so that you can adjust it when situations change. Consistency in following your roadmap is the key to success.

In the end, a structured life roadmap gives clarity, control, and confidence. It helps you move forward with purpose instead of confusion. When you follow a clear plan, your efforts become more focused, and you create a strong path toward a better and successful life.

Reviewing Life Goals Regularly

Reviewing life goals regularly is an important habit for staying on the right path in life. Many people set goals once but forget to check their progress later. Over time, this can lead to loss of focus and direction. When you review your goals regularly, you remind yourself what you are working for and make sure your actions are still aligned with your purpose. This habit keeps your mind clear and focused.

Regular review helps you understand what is working and what is not. Sometimes your efforts may not give the expected results, and without review, you may continue the same mistakes. But when you check your progress, you can identify problems early and make necessary changes. This improves your performance and helps you move forward in a better way.

Life situations and priorities can also change with time. What was important earlier may not have the same value now. Reviewing your goals helps you adjust them according to your current situation and future needs. This flexibility keeps your plan realistic and practical.

Another benefit of reviewing goals is that it increases motivation. When you see your progress, even small improvements, it builds confidence and encourages you to keep working. It also reminds you of how far you have come, which gives a sense of achievement and energy to continue.

A simple way to review your goals is to set a fixed time, like weekly or monthly. During this time, check what you have achieved, what challenges you faced, and what improvements are needed. Write down your thoughts and update your plan if required. This habit makes your journey more organized and effective.

In the end, reviewing life goals regularly helps you stay aware, focused, and flexible. It ensures that you are moving in the right direction and making progress toward your desired future. This simple habit can make a big difference in achieving success and building a well-planned life.

Making Adjustments When Necessary

Making adjustments when necessary is a practical skill that helps a person stay aligned with their goals. No plan works perfectly in every situation, and changes are a natural part of life. When individuals understand this, they become more open to improving their actions instead of feeling stuck. Adjusting plans at the right time helps them stay focused on results rather than being limited by one fixed method.

This habit also helps in better decision making. When a person observes their progress and notices that something is not working, they can take a step back and think clearly. Instead of repeating the same mistake, they choose a smarter way to move forward. This improves efficiency and helps them use their time and effort more wisely.

Adapting to change is a sign of growth and maturity. Life often brings unexpected situations, and a rigid mindset can create stress and confusion. But when a person learns to adjust their approach, they become more confident in handling challenges. This flexibility allows them to continue their journey without losing direction.

Making adjustments also strengthens learning and awareness. Every experience gives feedback, and this feedback is valuable for improvement. When individuals pay attention to outcomes, they understand what needs to be improved and what should be continued. This process builds better strategies and increases chances of success.

A helpful method is to review your actions regularly and compare them with your goals. If there is a gap, make small changes instead of big sudden shifts. Step-by-step improvement keeps the process simple and manageable. Over time, these small changes create strong progress.

This approach builds clarity, confidence, and better control over life decisions. It helps a person move forward with understanding, improve their path, and achieve goals with a more balanced and effective mindset.

Staying Committed to Personal Growth

Staying committed to personal growth means continuously working on yourself to become better in thinking, skills, and behavior. Growth does not happen in one day; it is a long process that requires patience, effort, and consistency. Many people start improving themselves with excitement, but they stop after some time when results are slow. True growth comes when a person remains committed even when progress is not immediately visible.

Commitment to growth helps a person build strong habits and discipline. When you decide to improve yourself daily, even in small ways, these small actions create big changes over time. Reading, learning new skills, improving communication, and developing positive habits all contribute to long-term success. This continuous effort makes a person stronger and more capable.

An important understanding is that personal growth is a lifelong journey. There is always something new to learn and improve. People who stay committed to growth do not become satisfied with small achievements; they keep learning and evolving. This mindset helps them stay ahead and adapt to changing situations in life and career.

Another valuable point is that growth requires stepping out of the comfort zone. A person must be ready to face challenges, try new things, and accept temporary discomfort. This is where real improvement happens. Comfort may feel easy, but growth comes from effort and learning.

Staying committed also means managing distractions and staying focused on your purpose. There will be many situations that try to pull your attention away, but discipline helps you stay on track. When you protect your time and energy, your growth becomes more consistent and effective.

This habit builds a strong mindset, improves confidence, and creates a clear path for future success. It helps a person become more capable, adaptable, and prepared to achieve higher goals in both personal and professional life.

Making Decisions Aligned with Your Blueprint

Making decisions aligned with your blueprint means choosing actions that match your long-term goals, values, and life plan. A blueprint is like a personal guide that shows what kind of life you want to build. When your decisions follow this blueprint, your efforts become focused and meaningful. Without this alignment, people often make random choices that may feel right in the moment but do not support their future growth.

This approach helps a person stay clear and confident in decision making. When you already know your goals and priorities, it becomes easier to say yes to the right opportunities and no to distractions. This saves time and energy and keeps you moving in the right direction without confusion.

An important understanding is that not every good opportunity is right for you. Some options may look attractive but do not match your long-term plan. When you follow your blueprint, you learn to choose what truly supports your growth instead of following temporary benefits. This thinking helps build a strong and disciplined mindset.

Making aligned decisions also improves consistency. When your daily actions match your bigger vision, you start building habits that support your goals. This creates steady progress and reduces the chances of going off track. Over time, these aligned actions bring strong and lasting results.

To understand this clearly, consider a person named Lemoon. Lemoon has a clear blueprint for his life. He knows the kind of career he wants, the skills he needs to develop, and the lifestyle he wants to build. Because of this clarity, he carefully chooses his actions. When he gets different opportunities, he checks if they match his long-term goals. If they do not support his growth, he avoids them, even if they seem easy or attractive. This discipline helps him stay focused and move forward with confidence.

This mindset builds clarity, focus, and strong decision-making ability. It helps a person avoid confusion, use time wisely, and stay committed to their path. When decisions are aligned with a clear blueprint, life becomes more organized and progress becomes more effective and purposeful.

Balancing Career, Health, and Relationships

Balancing career, health, and relationships is very important for a stable and successful life. Many people focus only on career growth and ignore their health and personal relationships. This creates stress, low energy, and emotional imbalance over time. True success is not only about earning money but also about living a healthy and peaceful life with strong relationships. When all three areas are balanced, a person feels more satisfied and performs better in every part of life.

Career growth is important, but it should not come at the cost of health. Good health gives energy, focus, and strength to work effectively. Simple habits like proper sleep, regular exercise, and a healthy diet can improve both physical and mental performance. Without good health, even success in career may not bring happiness or stability.

Relationships are equally important because they provide emotional support and happiness. Spending time with family and close people builds trust and connection. When relationships are strong, a person feels supported during difficult times and more confident in daily life. Ignoring relationships can lead to loneliness and stress, even if career success is achieved.

A practical approach to balance all three areas is time management. A person should plan their day in a way that includes work, health activities, and time for relationships. Even small efforts like daily exercise and regular communication with loved ones can create a big positive impact over time.

An important understanding is that balance does not mean giving equal time every day to everything, but it means giving the right attention at the right time. There may be periods where career needs more focus, but health and relationships should never be ignored completely.

This balanced approach creates a strong foundation for long-term success and happiness. It helps a person stay healthy, mentally stable, and emotionally connected while achieving their goals in a steady and meaningful way.

Living Intentionally Instead of Randomly

Living intentionally instead of randomly means making conscious choices about how you spend your time, energy, and focus. Many people live without clear thinking, reacting to situations and following habits without purpose. This leads to confusion, wasted effort, and slow progress. But when a person lives intentionally, every action is guided by clear goals, values, and priorities, which creates a more meaningful and focused life.

Intentional living helps a person take control of their decisions. Instead of doing things just because others are doing them, they choose actions that match their personal goals. This reduces distractions and increases productivity. It also helps in building a clear direction where every step supports long-term growth.

An important understanding is that small daily choices shape the future. What you do every day, how you think, and how you use your time slowly build your life. When you act without thinking, you may develop habits that do not support your goals. But when you act with intention, even small actions become powerful steps toward success.

Living intentionally also improves self-awareness. A person starts understanding what is truly important and what should be avoided. This awareness helps in better time management, stronger discipline, and more meaningful use of resources. It creates a life where actions are not random but planned and purposeful.

A practical way to live intentionally is to start your day with a clear plan. Decide your important tasks, avoid unnecessary distractions, and focus on completing meaningful work. At the end of the day, review your actions and check if they match your goals. This simple habit builds clarity and control over time.

This way of living creates focus, discipline, and long-term success. It helps a person avoid confusion, make better decisions, and build a life that is not based on chance but on clear purpose and thoughtful action.

6.

The Discipline Habit

Why Discipline is Stronger than Motivation

Discipline is stronger than motivation because it helps a person take action even when they do not feel like doing anything. Motivation is based on feelings, and feelings can change every day. But discipline is a decision to keep going no matter what. A person who depends only on motivation will stop when things become difficult, while a disciplined person continues working and moving forward.

Discipline creates a fixed routine, and routine builds success. When a person follows a daily schedule, their actions become automatic. They do not wait for the perfect time or mood. This consistency helps them complete their work regularly and improve step by step. Over time, these small consistent actions create strong results.

One important knowledge is that successful people are not always motivated, but they are always disciplined. They understand that progress comes from repeated effort, not from temporary excitement. Discipline helps a person control their mind, avoid distractions, and stay focused on long-term goals.

It also builds mental strength. When a person follows discipline daily, they learn to control laziness, fear, and distractions. This makes them stronger and more confident in handling challenges. Discipline trains the mind to act with responsibility instead of waiting for feelings.

To understand this clearly, look at the journey of a person named Peter. Peter had big dreams but struggled to stay consistent. In the beginning, he worked only when he felt motivated, and because of this, his progress was slow and irregular. One day, he decided to change his approach and focus on discipline instead of motivation. He created a simple daily routine and promised himself to follow it no matter how he felt.

Peter started waking up at a fixed time, working on his goals daily, and avoiding distractions. There were many days when he felt tired and unmotivated, but he still continued his routine. Slowly, his actions became a habit, and his work improved. Months passed, and Peter gained new skills, built confidence, and started achieving his goals. His success did not come from motivation, but from his daily discipline and consistency.

This journey shows that discipline is the real power behind long-term success. It helps a person stay consistent, build strong habits, and achieve goals with focus and control, even when motivation is not present.

Understanding How Habits Are Formed

Understanding how habits are formed helps a person take control of their daily actions and improve their life step by step. Habits are not created suddenly; they are built through repeated actions over time. When a person does the same activity again and again, the brain starts accepting it as a normal routine. This is why both good and bad habits become automatic if they are repeated regularly.

A simple way to understand habit formation is through three steps: cue, action, and reward. A cue is a trigger that starts the habit, the action is the behavior itself, and the reward is the benefit you feel after completing it. When this cycle repeats many times, the habit becomes strong and easy to follow. This knowledge helps a person build positive habits and remove negative ones.

Consistency plays the most important role in forming habits. It is not about doing something perfectly, but about doing it regularly. Even small actions, when repeated daily, can create powerful habits. For example, studying for a short time every day is more

effective than studying for long hours only once in a while.
Another important point is to start small and simple. Many people try to change everything at once, which becomes difficult to maintain. But when you start with small habits, they are easier to follow and slowly become part of your routine. Once a habit becomes stable, you can increase its level step by step.
Environment also affects habit formation. When your surroundings support your goals, it becomes easier to build good habits. For example, keeping your workspace clean or staying around focused people can help you stay disciplined. A good environment reduces distractions and supports positive behavior.
This understanding helps a person build strong and positive habits that support long-term success. It gives clarity on how actions become automatic and how small daily efforts can shape a better and more disciplined life.

Building Powerful Daily Routines

Building powerful daily routines helps a person create structure and consistency in life. A routine is a set of actions you follow every day, and it directly affects your productivity and success. When your daily routine is strong, you do not waste time deciding what to do next. Instead, you move with clarity and focus, which helps you complete important tasks efficiently.
A powerful routine is not about doing many things, but about doing the right things regularly. Simple habits like waking up on time, planning your day, working with focus, and taking care of your health can create big changes over time. These small actions, when repeated daily, build discipline and improve overall performance.
Consistency is the key to making any routine effective. Many people start with energy but stop after a few days. A strong routine is built when you follow it even on days when you do not feel motivated. This regular practice trains your mind to stay focused and committed to your goals.
Another important point is to keep your routine simple and

practical. A complicated routine is difficult to follow for a long time. Start with a few important habits and slowly improve your routine step by step. This makes it easier to stay consistent and avoid feeling overwhelmed.

Your routine should also include time for rest and health. Proper sleep, exercise, and short breaks are necessary to maintain energy and focus. A balanced routine helps you stay active and productive without feeling tired or stressed.

A well-designed daily routine creates discipline, saves time, and improves results. It helps a person stay focused, build strong habits, and move steadily toward their goals with clarity and control.

Replacing Negative Habits with Positive Ones

Replacing negative habits with positive ones is an important step toward improving life and achieving success. Negative habits slowly reduce productivity, confidence, and growth, while positive habits build discipline and progress. Many people try to stop bad habits suddenly, but this is difficult. A better approach is to replace them with better actions so that the mind does not feel empty or forced.

The first step is to identify your negative habits clearly. You need to understand what habits are stopping your progress, such as wasting time, delaying work, or unhealthy routines. Awareness is important because you cannot change what you do not understand. Once you know your habits, you can start working on them with a clear plan.

Instead of only trying to stop a bad habit, replace it with a useful one. For example, if you waste time on unnecessary activities, replace that time with learning a new skill or doing productive work. This method works better because your mind shifts focus instead of resisting change.

Consistency is very important in this process. Positive habits take time to build, and results may not be visible immediately. But when you repeat the right actions daily, they slowly become part of your routine. Over time, the new habit becomes stronger, and the old habit starts disappearing naturally.

Another important point is to control your environment. Remove triggers that lead to negative habits and create a space that supports positive actions. For example, keeping your workspace organized or staying away from distractions can make a big difference. Your surroundings play a strong role in shaping your behavior.

This process helps a person improve discipline, build better habits, and create a more productive lifestyle. It allows them to replace harmful patterns with useful actions and move forward with clarity, control, and steady personal growth.

Developing Self-Control and Consistency

Developing self-control and consistency is very important for achieving success and building a strong personality. Self-control means managing your thoughts, emotions, and actions, while consistency means doing the right things regularly. When both work together, a person can stay focused on their goals and avoid distractions that slow down progress.

Self-control helps a person make better decisions. In daily life, there are many temptations and distractions that can waste time and energy. When a person has strong self-control, they can avoid these distractions and choose actions that support their growth. This ability to control impulses is a key factor in long-term success.

Consistency is what turns small efforts into big results. Doing something once is not enough, but doing it daily creates real change. When a person works consistently, even small actions become powerful over time. This builds discipline and helps them move forward step by step without losing focus.

An important understanding is that self-control becomes stronger with practice. It is not something you are born with; it is something you develop over time. By making small disciplined choices daily, you train your mind to stay focused and avoid unnecessary habits. This strengthens your ability to stay committed to your goals.

A simple way to develop both qualities is to create a daily routine and follow it without excuses. Start with small tasks and complete them regularly. Avoid overloading yourself and focus on steady improvement. This makes it easier to stay consistent and build control over your actions.

This habit helps a person stay focused, improve discipline, and achieve goals with steady effort. It builds inner strength, reduces distractions, and creates a clear path toward a more productive and successful life.

The Importance of Daily Discipline in Success

Daily discipline is one of the most important factors in achieving success because it creates consistency in actions. Success is not the result of one big effort, but the result of small actions repeated every day. When a person follows discipline daily, they keep moving forward even when they do not feel motivated. This steady effort builds strong progress over time.

Discipline helps a person use time in the right way. Instead of wasting time on distractions, a disciplined person focuses on important tasks that bring real results. This improves productivity and allows them to complete more work in less time. Proper use of time is a major advantage in reaching goals faster.

Another important point is that daily discipline builds strong habits. When you follow a routine regularly, your actions become automatic. You do not need to force yourself again and again. This makes your work easier and more effective because your mind is trained to follow the right path.

Discipline also helps in difficult situations. There will be many days when things do not go as planned, and motivation is low. In such moments, discipline keeps you working. This ability to stay consistent during tough times is what separates successful people from others.

An important understanding is that discipline is built through small daily efforts. You do not need to make big changes at once. Start with simple tasks and complete them regularly. Over time, this builds strong control over your actions and creates long-term success.

This approach helps a person stay focused, improve performance, and achieve goals with confidence. Daily discipline creates stability, reduces distractions, and builds a strong foundation for a successful and productive life.

Creating Productive Morning Habits

Creating productive morning habits is very important because the way you start your day decides how the rest of your day will go. A focused and positive morning helps you stay energetic, clear, and ready to take action. When a person starts the day without planning, they often feel lazy and distracted, which affects their productivity. A strong morning routine builds discipline and sets the right tone for success.

Simple habits like waking up early, avoiding mobile use in the first hour, and planning your day can make a big difference. These small actions help your mind stay calm and focused. When you start your day with purpose, you feel more in control and ready to complete important tasks.

Morning time is best for high-value work because the mind is fresh and active. Using this time for learning, planning, or working on important goals increases efficiency. Instead of wasting this time on unproductive activities, using it wisely can improve your results significantly.

Health should also be part of your morning routine. Activities like light exercise, stretching, or a short walk improve blood flow and energy levels. A healthy start keeps your body active and your mind sharp throughout the day.

Another important point is consistency. A routine works only when you follow it daily. You do not need a complicated schedule; even a simple routine followed regularly can create powerful results. Over time, these habits become automatic and easier to follow. This practice builds focus, discipline, and positive energy for the entire day. It helps a person stay organized, use time wisely, and move closer to their goals with clarity and steady action.

Avoiding Distractions and Temptations

Avoiding distractions and temptations is very important for staying focused and achieving success. In today's world, there are many things that can easily take away attention, like mobile phones, social media, and unnecessary activities. When a person gets distracted often, their time and energy get wasted, and their progress becomes slow. Learning to control these distractions helps a person stay on the right path.

Distractions reduce productivity because they break concentration. When you keep switching between tasks, your mind takes time to refocus, which lowers the quality of work. A focused mind works faster and gives better results, so it is important to create an environment where distractions are limited.

One important understanding is that temptations are short-term pleasures that can harm long-term goals. For example, choosing entertainment over important work may feel good for a moment but can delay success. A disciplined person learns to control these urges and focuses on what truly matters for their future.

A practical way to avoid distractions is to set clear rules for yourself. You can fix specific times for using your phone, limit unnecessary apps, and create a clean workspace. Small steps like these help you stay focused and reduce unwanted interruptions.

Another helpful method is to plan your tasks in advance. When you know what you need to do, you are less likely to waste time thinking or getting distracted. A clear plan keeps your mind engaged and helps you complete work more efficiently.

This habit builds strong focus, better time management, and improved discipline. It helps a person stay committed to their goals, avoid unnecessary delays, and move forward with clear attention and steady progress.

Tracking Daily Habits for Improvement

Tracking daily habits is a powerful way to understand your progress and improve your life step by step. Many people work hard but do not track what they are doing, so they do not know where they are improving or where they are making mistakes. When you track your habits, you become more aware of your daily actions and how they affect your results. This awareness helps you stay focused and disciplined.

Habit tracking helps you stay consistent. When you write down or record your daily actions, you feel responsible to complete them. This creates a sense of commitment and encourages you to follow your routine regularly. Even simple tracking methods like marking a checklist or writing in a notebook can make a big difference.

Another important benefit is that it shows your real progress. Sometimes growth is slow and not visible, but when you track your habits, you can clearly see your improvement over time. This builds confidence and motivates you to continue your efforts without losing focus.

Tracking also helps in identifying weak areas. When you notice that certain habits are not followed regularly, you can understand the reason behind it and make changes. This allows you to improve your routine and remove actions that are not helping your growth.

A simple way to start is to choose a few important habits and track them daily. Do not try to track too many things at once. Keep it simple and focus on consistency. Over time, you can add more habits as you become comfortable with the process.

This practice builds discipline, awareness, and steady improvement. It helps a person stay focused on their goals, correct their mistakes, and create a more organized and productive daily routine.

Strengthening Willpower Through Practice

Strengthening willpower through practice is important for building self-control and achieving long-term goals. Willpower is the ability to control your actions, avoid distractions, and stay committed to what is important. Many people think willpower is natural, but it actually grows with regular practice and effort. When you train your mind daily, your ability to stay strong and focused improves.

Willpower becomes stronger when you take small disciplined actions every day. For example, completing tasks on time, avoiding unnecessary distractions, and following your routine builds mental strength. These small actions may look simple, but they train your brain to stay in control even in difficult situations.

One important understanding is that willpower is like a muscle. If you use it regularly, it becomes stronger, but if you ignore it, it becomes weak. This means you should practice self-control daily, even in small decisions. Over time, your mind becomes more powerful and stable.

Another key point is to avoid overloading yourself. Trying to control everything at once can make you feel tired and lose focus. It is better to start with one or two habits and improve them slowly. Step-by-step progress makes willpower stronger without creating pressure.

Creating a supportive environment also helps in strengthening willpower. When distractions are less and your surroundings support your goals, it becomes easier to stay focused. This reduces the need for constant control and makes your efforts more effective.

This practice builds strong self-control, better focus, and consistent action. It helps a person stay committed to their goals, handle challenges with confidence, and create steady progress toward a more disciplined and successful life.

Staying Disciplined During Difficult Situations

Staying disciplined during difficult situations is one of the most important qualities for long-term success. Easy days do not test a person, but tough situations show their real strength. When problems come, many people lose focus and stop working toward their goals. But a disciplined person continues their actions even when things are not going well. This ability helps them move forward while others give up.

Difficult situations can create stress, fear, and confusion, which can affect decision making. Discipline helps a person stay calm and focused instead of reacting emotionally. When you follow your routine even in tough times, you maintain control over your actions and avoid making wrong decisions.

An important understanding is that challenges are temporary, but the habits you build during those times can last forever. When you stay disciplined in hard situations, you train your mind to become stronger. This mental strength helps you handle future problems with more confidence and control.

It is helpful to focus on small actions during tough times. Instead of thinking about big results, concentrate on completing simple tasks daily. This keeps you moving forward and prevents you from feeling overwhelmed. Small steps can create progress even in difficult conditions.

Another important point is to maintain a positive and practical mindset. Accept that problems are part of life and focus on solutions instead of worrying too much. Discipline helps you stay consistent and take action even when motivation is low.

This quality builds resilience, strong character, and steady progress. It helps a person face challenges with confidence, stay committed to their goals, and continue growing even in difficult situations.

Making Discipline a Permanent Lifestyle

Making discipline a permanent lifestyle means turning good actions into daily habits that you follow without thinking. Discipline should not be used only for a short time; it should become part of your routine. When a person follows discipline regularly, their life becomes more organized, focused, and productive. Instead of depending on motivation, they build a system that supports continuous growth.

Discipline becomes permanent when it is simple and practical. Many people fail because they try to follow strict routines that are hard to maintain. It is better to start with small habits and follow them daily. Simple actions like waking up on time, planning your day, and completing important tasks can build a strong foundation over time.

Consistency is the key to making discipline a lifestyle. Doing the right thing every day, even in small amounts, creates long-term results. When actions are repeated daily, they become automatic and require less effort. This makes discipline easier and more natural.

Another important point is to create a system instead of relying on willpower. When your environment, routine, and schedule support your goals, it becomes easier to stay disciplined. For example, keeping a fixed time for work or removing distractions helps maintain consistency without extra effort.

It is also important to stay patient during this process. Discipline does not become permanent in a few days. It takes time, effort, and regular practice. When a person stays committed and does not give up, discipline slowly becomes a natural part of their life.

This approach builds strong habits, improves focus, and creates a stable path for success. It helps a person stay consistent, manage time effectively, and achieve goals with confidence and long-term control over their actions.

7.

Conquering Fear

Understanding the Psychology of Fear

Understanding the psychology of fear helps a person control their reactions and make better decisions in life. Fear is a natural emotion that protects us from danger, but many times it appears even when there is no real threat. It is often created by our thoughts, past experiences, or uncertainty about the future. When a person understands how fear works, they can handle it wisely instead of letting it control their actions.

Fear mainly comes from the unknown and the possibility of failure or loss. When the mind does not have clear information, it starts imagining negative outcomes. These thoughts increase anxiety and stop a person from taking action. This is why many people avoid opportunities, not because they are not capable, but because they are afraid of what might happen.

An important understanding is that fear becomes stronger when we avoid it. When a person keeps avoiding situations that create fear, the mind starts believing that the fear is real and dangerous. But when they face it step by step, the fear slowly reduces. Taking small actions helps build confidence and makes the mind stronger.

Fear can also be used in a positive way if managed properly. It can act as a signal that something is important and needs attention. Instead of running away, a person can prepare better, improve skills, and take careful action. This turns fear into a tool for growth instead of a barrier.

A practical way to manage fear is to understand the exact reason behind it. Ask yourself what you are really afraid of and whether it is real or just a thought. Breaking fear into smaller parts makes it easier to handle and reduces its intensity.

This understanding helps a person stay calm, think clearly, and take action even in uncertain situations. It builds confidence, reduces unnecessary stress, and allows steady progress toward goals with better control over thoughts and emotions.

Identifying Fears That Block Personal Growth

Identifying fears that block personal growth is important because many people fail not due to lack of ability but due to fear controlling their decisions. Fear of failure, fear of rejection, and fear of change can silently stop a person from taking action. When these fears are not identified, a person keeps avoiding opportunities and stays in the same position without growth. Understanding these fears is the first step to breaking them.

Fear mostly comes from negative thinking and imagining worst outcomes. The mind creates situations that may never happen, but still feels real. This stops a person from trying new things. An important knowledge is that fear grows stronger when we avoid it and becomes weaker when we face it with small actions.

To understand this clearly, consider the life of Harry Jorge. Harry Jorge had good skills and many chances to grow in his career, but he was always controlled by fear. He feared that if he tried something new, he might fail or people might judge him. Because of this, he kept saying no to opportunities and stayed in his comfort zone.

Harry Jorge avoided taking risks and preferred safe choices. Even when he had the ability to do better, his fear stopped him from moving forward. Over time, others who took action started growing, while Harry Jorge remained in the same place. His fear became a habit, and this habit slowly blocked his progress.

As years passed, Harry Jorge realized that his lack of growth was not due to lack of talent, but because he never faced his fears. He allowed fear to control his decisions, and this stopped him from becoming successful. He missed many chances that could have changed his life.

This example shows that fear can silently destroy progress if it is not identified and controlled. A person must recognize their fears, understand them, and take small steps to overcome them. Without this awareness, fear becomes a barrier that stops growth and success, even when the potential is high.

Fear of Failure and Its Impact on Success

Fear of failure is one of the biggest reasons why many people do not achieve success. It stops a person from taking action, trying new opportunities, and moving out of their comfort zone. Instead of focusing on growth, they focus on what might go wrong. This negative thinking creates hesitation and delays progress, even when the person has the ability to succeed.

Fear of failure affects decision making. When a person is afraid, they choose safe options instead of taking necessary risks. These safe choices may feel comfortable, but they do not lead to growth. Over time, this habit keeps a person stuck in the same position without improvement.

An important understanding is that failure is not the opposite of success, but a part of it. Every successful person has faced failure many times. Failure gives learning, experience, and clarity. When a person accepts this truth, their fear starts reducing, and they become more open to taking action.

Fear also reduces confidence. When a person keeps thinking about failure, they start doubting their own abilities. This self-doubt becomes a barrier and stops them from performing at their best. On the other hand, taking action builds confidence, even if the result is not perfect.

A practical way to overcome fear of failure is to take small steps. Instead of thinking about big results, focus on simple actions. Each small success builds confidence and reduces fear. This step-by-step approach makes progress easier and more manageable.

This understanding helps a person take action, learn from mistakes, and move forward with confidence. It removes hesitation, builds courage, and creates a mindset where failure is seen as a learning process, not a stopping point for success.

Learning to Face Uncertainty with Courage

Learning to face uncertainty with courage is very important because life is full of unknown situations. No one can predict the future completely, and waiting for perfect clarity often leads to delay and missed opportunities. A courageous person understands that uncertainty is a natural part of growth and chooses to move forward even without full guarantees.

Uncertainty creates fear because the mind wants safety and control. When things are not clear, the mind imagines negative outcomes. This stops many people from taking action. But courage means acting despite this fear, trusting that you will handle challenges as they come.

An important understanding is that growth always happens outside the comfort zone. When you try something new, there is always risk and uncertainty. But this is also where learning, improvement, and success take place. Avoiding uncertainty may feel safe, but it limits your potential.

Facing uncertainty becomes easier when you focus on preparation instead of fear. Improving your skills, gaining knowledge, and planning your actions give you confidence. Even if everything is not perfect, you feel ready to handle situations better.

Another helpful approach is to take small steps. You do not need to solve everything at once. Moving step by step reduces fear and builds confidence. Each action gives you more clarity and control over the situation.

This mindset helps a person stay strong, take smart risks, and move forward with confidence. It builds courage, reduces fear, and allows steady progress toward goals, even when the future is not fully clear.

Taking Calculated Risks in Life

Taking calculated risks in life is important for growth and success because without risk, progress becomes limited. A calculated risk means taking action after thinking carefully about possible outcomes instead of acting blindly. It is not about being careless, but about making smart decisions with proper understanding and planning.

Many people avoid risks because they fear loss or failure. But avoiding all risks also means missing opportunities that can change life. A person who learns to take calculated risks understands that some level of uncertainty is necessary for growth. They focus on learning and improving instead of only thinking about negative results.

An important understanding is that calculated risks are based on knowledge and preparation. Before taking a step, a person should gather information, understand the situation, and plan their actions. This reduces chances of failure and increases confidence in decision making.

Taking small risks first is a practical way to build confidence. Instead of making big decisions immediately, start with smaller actions. This helps you learn from experience and improve your ability to handle bigger challenges in the future.

Another key point is to accept that not every risk will give success, but every risk will give learning. Even if the result is not perfect, the experience helps you grow stronger and smarter. This mindset removes fear and encourages action.

This approach helps a person make better decisions, build confidence, and move forward with clarity. It allows them to take opportunities wisely, reduce fear, and create steady progress toward a more successful and fulfilling life.

Building Emotional Strength and Resilience

Building emotional strength and resilience is important for handling life's challenges with stability and confidence. Emotional strength means staying calm and balanced during difficult situations, while resilience means the ability to recover quickly from problems. Together, these qualities help a person face stress, failure, and pressure without losing control or direction.

In daily life, everyone faces ups and downs, but the difference is how they respond. A person with emotional strength does not react immediately with anger or fear. Instead, they think calmly and take practical decisions. This helps in solving problems more effectively and avoiding unnecessary mistakes.

An important understanding is that resilience is built through experience. Every challenge, failure, or difficult situation is an opportunity to grow stronger. When a person faces problems instead of avoiding them, their mind becomes more stable and confident. Over time, they develop the ability to handle bigger challenges easily.

Another key point is to manage emotions instead of suppressing them. Ignoring feelings can create stress, but understanding and controlling them helps in maintaining balance. Simple practices like taking a pause, thinking clearly, and focusing on solutions can improve emotional control.

Support systems also play an important role. Being around positive people and sharing thoughts with trusted individuals can reduce stress and improve emotional strength. A good environment helps a person stay stable and focused during tough times.

This quality helps a person stay strong, recover from setbacks, and move forward with confidence. It builds inner stability, improves decision making, and creates a strong mindset that supports long-term success and personal growth.

Overcoming Rejection and Criticism

Overcoming rejection and criticism is important for personal growth because every person faces it at some point in life. Rejection and criticism can feel painful, but they are not the end of progress. They are part of the journey that helps a person improve and become stronger. When a person learns to handle them properly, they turn into valuable lessons instead of obstacles.

Many people take rejection personally and start doubting their abilities. This creates fear and stops them from trying again. But an important understanding is that rejection is not always about your ability; sometimes it is about timing, situation, or different expectations. Knowing this helps reduce negative thinking and keeps confidence stable.

Criticism can be of two types: useful and useless. Useful criticism helps you improve by showing your mistakes, while useless criticism is often based on opinions without value. A smart person learns to accept useful feedback and ignore unnecessary negativity. This helps in improving without losing focus.

Another important point is to stay emotionally strong. Instead of reacting with anger or sadness, try to understand the reason behind rejection or criticism. This calm approach helps you learn from the situation and make better decisions in the future.

Taking action again is the key to overcoming rejection. When a person keeps trying despite setbacks, they build confidence and resilience. Each attempt makes them stronger and more experienced, bringing them closer to success.

This mindset helps a person stay confident, learn from feedback, and move forward without fear. It builds emotional strength, improves self-belief, and creates a positive approach toward challenges and personal growth.

Developing Confidence Through Action

Developing confidence through action is one of the most effective ways to build strong self-belief. Confidence does not come from thinking or waiting; it comes from doing. Many people wait to feel confident before taking action, but the truth is that confidence grows only after you take steps, even if they are small. Action creates experience, and experience builds confidence.

When a person takes action regularly, they start understanding their abilities better. Each completed task, even a small one, gives a sense of achievement. This positive feeling strengthens belief in oneself and reduces fear. Over time, repeated actions make a person more comfortable and capable in handling challenges.

An important understanding is that fear reduces only when you face it. If you keep avoiding situations, your confidence will never grow. But when you take action despite fear, your mind learns that the situation is not as difficult as it seemed. This process slowly removes hesitation and builds courage.

Another key point is to start small and stay consistent. You do not need to take big steps in the beginning. Simple actions done daily are enough to create progress. As you become comfortable, you can increase the level of difficulty and take bigger steps.

It is also important to focus on progress, not perfection. Many people lose confidence because they expect perfect results. Instead, learning from each action and improving step by step builds stronger and long-lasting confidence.

This approach helps a person take control of their life, reduce fear, and build real confidence. It creates a mindset of action, encourages continuous growth, and supports success through steady effort and practical experience.

Transforming Fear into Motivation

Transforming fear into motivation is a powerful skill that can change a person's life direction. Fear is not always negative; it can also be a signal that something important needs attention. Instead of running away from fear, a smart person learns to use it as energy to take action. When fear is understood properly, it becomes a driving force rather than a barrier.

Fear often shows areas where growth is needed. For example, fear of failure may mean that the goal is important, and fear of public speaking may show the need to improve communication skills. When a person sees fear as a guide instead of a problem, they start working on improvement instead of avoiding the situation.

An important understanding is that fear creates strong emotional energy. If this energy is directed in the right way, it can increase focus and determination. Instead of wasting energy on worry, using it for preparation and action can lead to better results. This shift in thinking is the key to turning fear into motivation.

A practical way to do this is to break fear into small steps. When a situation feels too big, it creates pressure. But when you divide it into simple actions, it becomes easier to handle. Each small step reduces fear and builds confidence, which increases motivation to continue.

Another key point is to focus on purpose instead of fear. When your goal is clear and meaningful, it becomes stronger than your fear. This helps you take action even when you feel uncomfortable. Purpose gives direction, and fear becomes a tool that pushes you forward.

This approach helps a person use fear in a positive way, build courage, and stay motivated. It creates a mindset where challenges are seen as opportunities, and fear becomes a source of energy for growth and success.

Breaking Mental Barriers That Limit Progress

Breaking mental barriers that limit progress is important for achieving real growth in life. Mental barriers are negative thoughts, beliefs, and fears that stop a person from taking action. These barriers are not real obstacles, but they feel real because the mind accepts them as truth. When a person understands this, they can start working on changing their thinking.

Many people believe statements like "I am not capable," "I cannot do this," or "this is too difficult." These thoughts create limits and reduce confidence. An important understanding is that these beliefs are often based on past experiences or fear, not on actual ability. When a person questions these thoughts, they start seeing new possibilities.

Breaking mental barriers requires awareness and action. First, a person must identify the negative beliefs that are stopping them. Then, they should replace them with positive and realistic thoughts. For example, instead of thinking "I cannot do this," they can think "I can learn and improve." This small change in thinking can create a big difference.

Taking action is the most powerful way to break these barriers. When a person takes small steps, they prove to themselves that they are capable. Each action reduces fear and builds confidence. Over time, the mind becomes stronger and more open to challenges.

Another key point is to stay consistent and patient. Mental barriers are built over time, so they also take time to break. Regular effort, positive thinking, and continuous action help in removing these limits slowly but surely.

This process helps a person unlock their true potential, build confidence, and move forward without fear. It creates a strong mindset, removes self-doubt, and allows steady progress toward success and personal growth.

Living Boldly Beyond Fear

Living boldly beyond fear means choosing to take action even when you feel afraid. Fear is a natural part of life, but it should not control your decisions or limit your growth. A bold person understands that fear will always be there, but still moves forward with courage and clear purpose. This mindset helps a person explore opportunities and live a more meaningful life.

Many people stay stuck because they wait for fear to disappear before taking action. But the truth is, fear does not go away completely. It reduces only when you face it. When you start taking small steps despite fear, your confidence grows and your mind becomes stronger. This is how boldness is developed over time.

An important understanding is that bold actions create new experiences and open doors for success. When you step out of your comfort zone, you learn new skills, meet new challenges, and discover your true potential. Avoiding fear may feel safe, but it keeps life limited and predictable.

Another key point is to focus on what you can control. Instead of worrying about outcomes, focus on your effort and preparation. When you give your best and stay consistent, results will improve naturally. This approach reduces fear and increases confidence in your actions.

It is also helpful to accept that mistakes are part of the journey. A bold person does not aim for perfection but focuses on learning and improving. Each mistake becomes a lesson that makes them stronger and wiser.

This way of living helps a person break limits, build courage, and move forward with confidence. It creates a powerful mindset where fear no longer controls life, and growth becomes a continuous and rewarding journey.

8:

The Art of Focus

Understanding the Importance of Focus in Success

Understanding the importance of focus in success is essential because focus decides how effectively a person uses their time and energy. Without focus, even hard work does not give proper results. A focused person knows what is important and avoids unnecessary distractions, which helps them move faster toward their goals. Focus is not about doing many things, but about doing the right things with full attention.

Many people struggle because their attention is divided between too many tasks. This reduces quality and slows progress. An important knowledge is that focus increases productivity and improves decision making. When the mind is clear and concentrated, a person can complete tasks faster and with better results.

To understand this deeply, consider the journey of James, a boy from a middle-class family. James had big dreams, but his life was full of distractions like social media, unnecessary outings, and lack of direction. Because of this, he was not able to perform well in studies or improve his skills. He realized that without focus, his future would not change.

James decided to improve his focus step by step. First, he reduced distractions by limiting phone use and creating a fixed study time. Then, he started setting clear daily goals and worked on one task at a time. Slowly, his concentration improved, and he began understanding things better.

As months passed, James became more disciplined and focused.

His results started improving, and he gained confidence in his abilities. He used his time wisely, learned new skills, and stayed consistent with his efforts. His focus helped him move ahead of others who were still distracted.

In the future, James continued this habit and achieved success in his career. His focused mindset helped him take better decisions, grow professionally, and support his family. This shows that focus is a powerful tool that can change life step by step. It helps a person stay clear, work efficiently, and achieve long-term success with strong direction and purpose.

The Science Behind Concentration

The science behind concentration explains how the brain focuses on one task at a time to give better results. The human brain is not designed to handle many tasks together effectively. When a person tries to do multiple things, the brain keeps shifting attention, which reduces speed and quality of work. Concentration improves when full attention is given to a single task without distractions.

Concentration depends on mental energy and clarity. When the mind is fresh, focus becomes strong, but when it is tired or stressed, concentration becomes weak. That is why proper sleep, short breaks, and a healthy routine are important. A calm environment also helps the brain stay focused for a longer time.

An important understanding is that concentration can be trained like a skill. When a person practices focusing daily, even for a short time, the brain becomes stronger. Over time, it becomes easier to stay focused and avoid distractions naturally.

Distractions are the biggest enemy of concentration. Mobile phones, social media, and unnecessary thoughts reduce focus and waste time. Controlling these distractions and creating a clear workspace can improve concentration quickly and effectively.

Another useful method is to work in small time blocks. Focusing for 25–30 minutes and then taking a short break helps the brain stay active and avoid tiredness. This method keeps concentration

steady and improves productivity.
This understanding helps a person improve focus, work efficiently, and use their time wisely. It builds strong attention, reduces mistakes, and supports better performance in studies, work, and daily life.

Identifying Common Distractions in Modern Life

Identifying common distractions in modern life is important because distractions reduce focus and slow down progress. Today, many people struggle not because of lack of ability, but because their attention is divided. Mobile phones, social media, constant notifications, and unnecessary internet use are some of the biggest distractions that take away valuable time.
One major issue is that these distractions look small but consume a lot of time daily. Checking your phone for a few minutes again and again can turn into hours of lost productivity. This habit breaks concentration and makes it difficult to complete important tasks with full focus.
Another common distraction is overthinking and negative thoughts. Sometimes, the biggest distraction is not outside but inside the mind. Worrying about past mistakes or future problems reduces mental clarity and stops a person from focusing on present work.
An important understanding is that distractions reduce both quality and speed of work. When focus is broken, it takes time for the brain to return to the same level of concentration. This results in more time spent and less output achieved.
A practical way to handle distractions is to identify them clearly and reduce their access. For example, keeping the phone away while working, turning off unnecessary notifications, and setting a fixed time for social media can improve focus. Creating a clean and quiet workspace also supports better concentration.
This awareness helps a person take control of their time, improve focus, and work more effectively. It builds discipline, reduces

unnecessary interruptions, and creates a strong habit of staying focused on important goals.

The Power of Prioritizing Tasks

The power of prioritizing tasks helps a person focus on what truly matters and avoid wasting time on less important work. In daily life, there are many tasks, but not all tasks give the same result. A smart person understands which tasks are important and gives them priority. This helps in achieving better results with less stress and more clarity.

Many people stay busy the whole day but still feel unproductive because they do not set clear priorities. They spend time on easy or unimportant tasks while delaying important work. This habit reduces progress and creates pressure at the end. Prioritizing tasks solves this problem by giving clear direction.

An important understanding is that not every task needs equal attention. Some tasks have high impact and should be completed first. Focusing on these important tasks increases productivity and helps in achieving goals faster. This is often called working smart instead of just working hard.

A practical way to prioritize is to make a simple list of tasks and mark them as important, less important, and optional. Starting your day with the most important task builds momentum and increases confidence. It also ensures that key work is completed on time.

Another key point is to avoid multitasking. When you focus on one important task at a time, your quality of work improves and you complete it faster. This also reduces mental stress and keeps your mind clear.

This approach helps a person stay organized, manage time effectively, and achieve better results. It creates clarity, improves focus, and supports steady progress toward personal and professional success.

Practicing Single-Tasking Instead of Multitasking

Practicing single-tasking instead of multitasking is a powerful way to improve focus and get better results in less time. Many people think doing many things together makes them faster, but it actually reduces efficiency. When the mind keeps switching between tasks, it loses clarity and energy. Single-tasking helps the brain stay calm and work with full attention on one task.

When a person focuses on one task, they understand it more deeply and complete it with better quality. This also reduces mistakes and saves time that is usually wasted in correcting errors. A clear focus brings better results and creates a sense of satisfaction after completing the work.

A valuable insight is that attention is limited. If it is divided, performance becomes weak. But when attention is fully used on one task, productivity increases naturally. This makes work easier and less stressful.

A simple method to practice single-tasking is to create a clear work plan. Decide what task to do, remove distractions, and give your full attention until it is finished. Even small habits like keeping your phone away and working in a quiet place can make a big difference.

Another helpful approach is to train your mind slowly. Start by focusing on one task for a short time, like 20–30 minutes, and then increase the duration. This builds mental strength and improves your ability to stay focused for longer periods.

This practice helps a person build strong concentration, improve work quality, and manage time better. It creates a disciplined mindset, reduces confusion, and supports steady progress in both personal and professional life.

Creating a Distraction-Free Work Environment

A focused workspace is not only about removing noise, but also about controlling what enters your mind while working. When you sit to do important work, your brain should feel clear and ready, not overloaded with random thoughts or outside disturbances. A well-managed space helps your mind stay steady and improves the quality of your thinking.

One powerful way to improve focus is to prepare your workspace before starting. Keep everything ready so you do not need to get up again and again. This simple habit keeps your flow active and prevents loss of concentration during important tasks.

Your mental environment also matters as much as your physical space. If your mind is full of stress or too many thoughts, it becomes difficult to focus. Taking a few minutes to relax your mind before starting work can improve your attention and clarity.

Another useful idea is to set clear boundaries for your work time. Treat your work time seriously and avoid mixing it with entertainment or casual activities. When you respect your work time, your mind also learns to stay focused during that period.

It is also helpful to plan short breaks in between work. Continuous work without rest can reduce focus, but small breaks refresh the mind and help you return with better energy. This balance keeps your productivity stable throughout the day.

This method helps a person stay mentally clear, work with full attention, and avoid unnecessary interruptions. It builds strong focus habits, improves thinking ability, and supports better results in both personal and professional tasks.

Managing Digital Distractions Effectively

Digital distractions are one of the biggest reasons for loss of focus in today's life. Mobile phones, social media, and constant online activity can easily take away hours without giving real value. To stay productive, a person must learn to control technology instead of being controlled by it. This awareness itself is the first step toward better focus and time management.

A smart approach is to use digital tools with purpose. Before opening any app or website, decide why you are using it. This small habit reduces random scrolling and helps you stay focused on useful tasks. When your usage has a clear reason, your time becomes more valuable.

Another important step is to create fixed time slots for using digital platforms. Instead of checking your phone again and again, decide specific times for messages and social media. This keeps your mind free during work and reduces unnecessary interruptions.

It is also helpful to remove or limit apps that waste time. If an app is not helping in growth or learning, reducing its use can improve focus quickly. Keeping only important tools on your device creates a cleaner digital space.

A strong practice is to start your day without immediately using your phone. When you begin your day with clear thinking instead of digital noise, your focus remains better throughout the day. This simple habit can create a big positive change in your daily routine.

This approach helps a person stay in control of their time, improve concentration, and use technology wisely. It builds discipline, reduces mental overload, and supports steady progress in work and personal development.

Using Time Blocks to Improve Productivity

Time blocking is a simple method where you divide your day into fixed time periods and assign each block to a specific task. This approach helps you stay organized and reduces confusion about what to do next. When your day is already planned in blocks, you spend less time deciding and more time doing important work.

This method works because it gives clear direction to your mind. Instead of jumping between tasks, you stay focused on one activity for a fixed time. This improves the quality of your work and helps you complete tasks faster. It also reduces mental pressure because everything is already structured.

A useful way to apply this is to match your energy levels with your tasks. Do your most important work when your mind is fresh, and keep lighter tasks for later. This helps you use your energy in a smart way and increases overall performance.

Another helpful idea is to keep small gaps between blocks. These short breaks give your mind time to relax and prepare for the next task. This keeps your focus strong and prevents tiredness during long working hours.

It is also important to follow your time blocks with discipline. Avoid changing tasks in between unless it is necessary. When you respect your schedule, your mind becomes more trained and focused over time.

This approach helps a person manage time better, stay organized, and improve work quality. It builds strong focus habits, reduces stress, and supports steady progress toward daily and long-term goals.

Practicing Mindfulness for Better Concentration

Mindfulness is the practice of giving full attention to the present moment without getting lost in past or future thoughts. When a person trains their mind to stay in the present, concentration improves naturally. Many times, lack of focus happens because the mind keeps wandering, not because the task is difficult.

A simple way to build this habit is to observe your thoughts without reacting to them. When your mind starts thinking about something else, gently bring your attention back to the work. This repeated practice slowly trains your brain to stay focused for longer periods.

One important idea is that focus becomes strong when the mind is calm. If the mind is filled with stress or overthinking, it becomes difficult to concentrate. Taking a few minutes to sit quietly, breathe slowly, and relax your thoughts can improve your attention before starting any work.

Another helpful step is to stay fully involved in whatever you are doing. Whether it is studying, working, or even a small task, give your complete attention without thinking about other things. This habit builds deep focus and improves the quality of your work.

It is also useful to reduce mental overload by doing one task at a time with full awareness. When you stay present, your mind becomes sharper and more clear, which helps in better understanding and faster learning.

This practice helps a person control their thoughts, improve concentration, and stay mentally strong. It builds inner calmness, increases clarity, and supports better performance in both daily life and long-term goals.

Strengthening Attention Through Mental Exercises

Improving attention is possible when you train your brain regularly with simple mental exercises. Just like the body becomes strong with physical exercise, the mind also becomes sharp with practice. When you challenge your brain daily, your ability to focus and think clearly increases step by step.

A simple way to start is by doing activities that require full attention, such as reading carefully, solving puzzles, or remembering small details. These activities force your brain to stay active and improve concentration over time. Even spending a few minutes daily on such tasks can create a strong impact.

One useful idea is to practice deep thinking. Instead of quickly moving from one topic to another, try to stay on one idea and understand it properly. This builds patience and improves your ability to focus for a longer time without getting distracted.

Another helpful method is to train your memory. Try to recall what you studied, what you did during the day, or important points from a conversation. This improves brain activity and helps your mind stay alert and focused.

It is also important to increase your focus time slowly. Start with short periods of full attention and gradually increase the duration. This builds mental strength and makes it easier to concentrate on longer tasks without feeling tired.

This practice helps a person improve attention, think clearly, and work more effectively. It builds a sharp mind, reduces distractions, and supports better learning and performance in daily life.

Maintaining Focus During Long Projects

Working on long projects can be challenging because it requires patience and continuous effort over time. Many people start with full energy but lose focus in the middle. To maintain focus, it is important to break the project into smaller parts so that each step feels easy and achievable. This keeps motivation steady and reduces pressure.

When you divide a big task into small goals, your mind feels more clear and organized. Completing each small part gives a sense of progress, which helps you stay consistent. This also makes the overall project less stressful and more manageable.

One important idea is to keep your purpose clear. When you remind yourself why you started, it becomes easier to stay focused even when the work feels difficult. A strong reason gives energy to continue without giving up.

Another helpful step is to review your progress regularly. Checking what you have completed and what is left gives direction and helps you stay on track. This habit keeps your focus connected to your goal.

It is also useful to manage your energy, not just your time. Take proper rest, eat well, and keep your mind fresh. A tired mind cannot focus for long, so maintaining your energy is important for long-term work.

This approach helps a person stay consistent, complete long projects successfully, and avoid losing focus in the middle. It builds patience, improves discipline, and supports steady progress toward bigger goals.

Avoiding Burnout Through Balanced Focus

Working continuously without proper balance can lead to burnout, where both mind and body feel tired and lose interest in work. To avoid this, it is important to focus in a balanced way instead of pushing yourself too hard all the time. When you manage your effort wisely, you can stay productive for a longer period without feeling exhausted.

A smart approach is to mix focused work with proper rest. Giving your full attention during work time is important, but taking short breaks helps your mind recover and stay fresh. This balance keeps your energy stable and improves overall performance.

One useful idea is to listen to your body and mind. If you feel tired or stressed, it is a signal to slow down and take rest. Ignoring these signals can reduce your efficiency and lead to long-term problems. Paying attention to your energy helps you work better.

A helpful step is to avoid overloading yourself with too many tasks. Taking limited and realistic work keeps your mind clear and prevents unnecessary pressure. When your workload is controlled, your focus becomes stronger and more stable.

It is also important to include activities that relax your mind, like walking, light exercise, or spending time in silence. These small habits refresh your thinking and help you return to work with better focus.

This approach helps a person stay active, avoid mental tiredness, and maintain steady focus in daily life. It builds a healthy routine, improves productivity, and supports long-term growth without stress or burnout.

Training the Brain for Deep Work

Deep work means doing a task with full concentration for a long time without distraction. It is a skill that can be developed with regular practice. In today's fast world, the brain gets used to quick and short attention, so it becomes important to train it again for deep and focused thinking.

A good way to start is by creating fixed time for focused work every day. Even 30 to 60 minutes of full concentration without interruption can improve your ability slowly. When you repeat this daily, your brain starts adapting to longer focus periods.

One strong idea is to reduce quick rewards like constant checking of phone or switching tasks. These habits make the brain restless and reduce patience. When you control these habits, your mind becomes more stable and ready for deep thinking.

Another helpful method is to set clear goals before starting work. When you know exactly what you want to complete, your mind stays directed and does not wander. Clear goals make your focus stronger and more effective.

It is also important to accept that deep focus feels difficult in the beginning. Your mind may try to escape, but staying committed during this phase builds mental strength. Over time, this discomfort reduces and focus becomes natural.

This practice helps a person think clearly, work with high quality, and achieve better results in less time. It builds strong concentration, improves problem-solving ability, and supports long-term success in both personal and professional life.

Improving Productivity with Focused Effort

Improving productivity with focused effort means using your time and energy in a smart and planned way instead of just working for long hours. Many people believe that working more time gives better results, but real productivity comes when your mind is fully engaged in the task. When you work with full attention, your brain processes information faster, reduces mistakes, and completes work with better quality. This saves both time and effort in the long run.

A strong understanding is that clarity increases productivity. When you clearly know what needs to be done, your mind does not get confused or distracted. Starting your work with a clear goal and proper direction helps you stay on track and avoid unnecessary actions. This makes your effort more powerful and effective.

An important point is to manage your mental energy, not just your time. Your brain works best when it is fresh and active. Doing important tasks during your peak energy time helps you complete work faster and with better results. Ignoring your energy levels can lead to slow work and low performance.

A useful idea is to focus on output instead of effort. Many people stay busy but do not produce meaningful results. Focused effort means giving importance to tasks that create real progress. When you work on high-value tasks, your productivity increases naturally without extra pressure.

It is also helpful to remove internal distractions like overthinking and self-doubt. These mental blocks reduce your speed and confidence. When you focus on action and keep your thinking simple, your work becomes smoother and more efficient.

Consistency plays a key role in improving productivity. Small focused efforts done daily create strong results over time. When you stay regular and disciplined, your mind becomes trained to work with focus, and productivity becomes a habit instead of a struggle.

This approach helps a person work with clarity, improve efficiency, and achieve better results without feeling stressed. It builds a strong mindset, increases work quality, and supports long-term success with smart and focused effort.

Maintaining Focus on Long-Term Goals

Maintaining focus on long-term goals requires strong control over your thoughts and actions because results do not come immediately. Many people lose direction when they do not see quick success, but staying focused means trusting your effort even when progress feels slow. A clear vision of your future keeps your mind steady and helps you continue without losing confidence.

A helpful approach is to break your long-term goal into smaller targets. When you achieve small steps, your mind feels progress and stays motivated. This also makes big goals feel easier and less stressful. Step-by-step progress keeps your focus strong and consistent.

Discipline is more important than motivation in long-term success. Motivation can change, but discipline keeps you working even on days when you do not feel like it. When you follow a routine, your mind becomes trained to stay focused without depending on mood. A useful idea is to protect your time from activities that do not support your goal. Every action should have a purpose. When you use your time wisely, your progress becomes faster and more meaningful.

It is also important to stay mentally strong during challenges. Difficult situations and delays are part of the journey. Instead of getting distracted or discouraged, staying calm and continuing your effort helps you move forward.

This method helps a person stay committed, avoid distractions, and move with clear direction. It builds patience, strengthens consistency, and supports steady progress toward meaningful success.

9.

Small Steps, Big Results

Understanding the Power of Consistent Action

Understanding the power of consistent action means realizing that small efforts done daily can create big results over time. Many people wait for perfect timing or big opportunities, but real progress comes from regular action. When a person keeps working step by step without stopping, success becomes more certain and stable.

Consistency builds momentum. When you take action every day, your mind and body get used to the process. This reduces laziness and increases discipline. Even on low-energy days, small actions keep you moving forward and prevent you from losing progress.

A strong idea is that consistency is more powerful than intensity. Doing a little work daily is better than doing a lot of work once and then stopping. Regular effort builds skills, improves understanding, and creates long-term results that last.

To understand this clearly, look at the journey of Charles, a boy from a middle-class family in the USA. Charles had big dreams but no special talent in the beginning. Instead of waiting for success, he decided to take small actions every day. He studied regularly, improved his skills slowly, and stayed consistent even when results were not visible.

In the first stage of his life, Charles focused on learning basic skills and building strong habits. He avoided distractions and followed a daily routine. In the next stage, his consistent effort started showing results. He became better than others who were not regular, and his confidence increased.

In the future, Charles continued this habit and achieved success step by step. His steady actions helped him build a strong career, improve his financial condition, and support his family. His story shows that consistency creates growth, even without perfect conditions.

This understanding helps a person stay regular, avoid giving up, and move forward with patience. It builds strong habits, improves discipline, and supports long-term success through simple and steady effort.

The Compound Effect of Small Improvements

The compound effect of small improvements means that tiny positive changes done regularly can create big success over time. Many people ignore small efforts because results are not immediate, but these small steps slowly build a strong foundation. When you improve even a little every day, the results start multiplying in the long run.

A clear understanding is that growth is not always visible in the beginning. Just like saving a small amount daily grows into a large amount, your skills and knowledge also increase with consistent improvement. Patience is important because real results appear after continuous effort.

Small improvements help in building strong habits. When you focus on becoming slightly better each day, your mind stays active and positive. This removes pressure and makes the journey easier to follow. Over time, these small habits create big changes in your performance.

A useful idea is to track your daily progress. When you see even small growth, it gives confidence and keeps you motivated. This helps you stay consistent and avoid losing direction during slow phases.

It is also important to avoid negative habits because they also grow with time. Just like positive actions give good results, small negative actions can create problems later. Being aware of your

daily choices helps you stay on the right path.
This concept helps a person stay patient, improve step by step, and achieve meaningful success. It builds discipline, increases growth, and supports long-term progress through simple and regular actions.

Why Small Habits Lead to Big Achievements

Small habits may look simple, but they have a strong impact on long-term success. When a person repeats a positive action daily, it slowly becomes part of their lifestyle. These daily actions build discipline and shape behaviour, which directly affects future results. Big achievements are not created in one day, they are built through regular effort.
A clear understanding is that habits control direction. What you do daily decides where you will reach in life. Even a small habit like reading, learning, or practicing a skill every day can create a big difference over time. Consistency in small actions brings steady progress without pressure.
Small habits reduce the difficulty of starting. When a task feels easy, the mind is more willing to do it regularly. This helps in building a routine that continues for a long time. Over time, these simple actions turn into strong skills and better performance.
A useful idea is to focus on improvement, not perfection. Trying to be perfect can create stress and stop action, but improving little by little keeps the process smooth and continuous. This mindset helps you stay active and grow without fear.
It is also important to stay patient because results take time to appear. Many people stop because they do not see quick success, but those who continue with small habits reach bigger goals in the future.
This understanding helps a person build strong routines, stay consistent, and achieve meaningful success. It improves discipline, increases growth, and supports long-term achievements through simple daily actions.

Avoiding the Trap of Perfectionism

Perfectionism may look like a good quality, but it often stops progress instead of improving it. Many people delay their work because they want everything to be perfect, but this habit creates fear and reduces action. Real growth comes when you start and improve along the way instead of waiting for perfect conditions.

A clear understanding is that progress matters more than perfection. When you focus on completing your work, you gain experience and learn faster. Mistakes become part of learning, and each step helps you move forward with better understanding.

Perfectionism increases pressure and makes simple tasks feel difficult. When your mind keeps looking for flaws, it becomes harder to take action. Letting go of this mindset helps you work freely and complete tasks with confidence.

A useful idea is to set realistic standards instead of perfect ones. When your goals are practical, your mind feels relaxed and ready to act. This helps in building consistency and keeps your work moving without unnecessary delay.

It is also important to accept that improvement happens step by step. No one becomes perfect in the beginning. Taking action, learning from results, and improving gradually creates better outcomes over time.

This approach helps a person take action without fear, complete work on time, and grow with experience. It builds confidence, reduces stress, and supports steady progress in both personal and professional life.

Learning Patience During Long Progress

Learning patience during long progress is important because meaningful results take time and steady effort. Many people feel frustrated when they do not see quick changes, but real growth happens slowly and quietly. When you understand this, your mind becomes calm and you continue your work without losing hope.

A clear understanding is that slow progress is still progress. Even if results are small, they are taking you forward. Accepting this truth helps you stay positive and keeps your focus strong during long journeys.

Impatience often leads to quitting or changing direction again and again. This breaks consistency and delays success. Staying patient helps you stick to one path and build strong results over time.

A useful idea is to focus on daily effort instead of final results. When your attention is on what you can do today, your mind feels relaxed and active. This reduces stress and improves your ability to continue for a long time.

It is also important to trust the process. Every step you take adds value, even if it is not visible immediately. Believing in your efforts gives you strength to keep moving forward.

This approach helps a person stay calm, avoid frustration, and continue working with stability. It builds strong mindset, improves consistency, and supports long-term success through steady and patient effort.

Improving Gradually Every Day

Improving gradually every day is a powerful way to achieve long-term success because it focuses on steady growth instead of sudden change. Many people try to improve quickly and take big steps, but they often lose consistency after some time. Small daily improvement is easier to maintain and builds a strong base for future success. When you improve even 1% every day, the result becomes very strong over months and years.

A clear understanding is that growth is a continuous process, not a one-time effort. Every small action you take adds value to your skills, knowledge, and mindset. These small steps may not show results immediately, but they create a strong foundation that leads to bigger achievements later. Patience is important because real change takes time to develop.

Daily improvement also helps in building self-discipline. When you commit to improving every day, your mind becomes trained to follow a routine. This reduces laziness and increases your ability to take action regularly. Over time, this discipline becomes a natural part of your life and helps you stay consistent in all areas.

A useful idea is to focus on learning and refining your actions. Instead of repeating the same effort, try to understand what can be done better. This habit of self-correction improves your efficiency and helps you grow faster without increasing pressure.

Another important point is to avoid comparing your progress with others. Everyone has a different journey, and comparing can create confusion and self-doubt. Focusing on your own improvement keeps your mind clear and helps you move forward with confidence.

It is also helpful to review your progress at regular intervals. Looking back at your growth shows how far you have come and keeps you motivated. This awareness strengthens your belief in the process and encourages you to continue your efforts.

This approach helps a person develop strong habits, improve step by step, and achieve meaningful results over time. It builds patience, increases confidence, and supports long-term success through consistent and focused daily improvement.

Tracking Small Improvements

Tracking small improvements helps you understand your real progress and keeps your mind focused on growth. Many times, people feel they are not improving because they do not notice small changes. When you track your daily actions, you can clearly see how your effort is moving you forward step by step. This builds confidence and removes self-doubt.

A clear understanding is that what gets measured gets improved. When you keep a record of your work, habits, or learning, your mind becomes more serious and responsible. It creates awareness about your actions and helps you stay consistent with your efforts.

Tracking also helps you identify what is working and what is not. When you observe your daily results, you can make better decisions and adjust your actions. This makes your growth more smart and effective instead of random effort.

A useful idea is to keep your tracking simple. You can use a notebook or a basic list to record your daily progress. The goal is not perfection, but regular awareness. Simple tracking is easy to follow and gives long-term benefits.

It is also helpful to review your progress weekly or monthly. Looking back at your journey shows your improvement and keeps you motivated. It also helps you stay connected with your goals and direction.

This habit helps a person stay aware, improve regularly, and build strong discipline. It increases clarity, strengthens consistency, and supports steady progress toward meaningful success.

10.

The Strength of Resilience

Realizing That True Strength Comes from How You Rise After Falling

Freed was an ordinary person who believed that strength meant never failing. In his early life, he tried to avoid risks because he was afraid of making mistakes. But this thinking kept him stuck in the same place, without growth or confidence. His life began to change when he faced a situation where failure was unavoidable. One day, Freed lost an important opportunity that he had worked for. He felt disappointed and questioned his ability. At that moment, he had two choices: to give up or to learn. Slowly, he understood that failure is not the opposite of success, but a part of it. This understanding became the turning point in his life.

Freed started observing his mistakes instead of ignoring them. He asked himself what went wrong and how he could improve. This habit helped him gain knowledge and clarity. Instead of feeling weak, he began to feel more aware and prepared for the future.

As time passed, Freed faced more challenges, but his reaction changed. He stopped fearing failure and started accepting it as a process. Each setback made him mentally stronger and more confident. He realized that real strength is built when a person continues after falling.

Freed also learned to control his emotions during tough times. Earlier, he used to feel frustrated and lose focus, but now he stayed calm and patient. This helped him make better decisions and move forward with a clear mind.

With this mindset, Freed slowly started achieving small successes. These wins were not sudden, but they were meaningful because they were built on learning and effort. His confidence grew, and he became more consistent in his actions.

Over time, Freed became a stronger person, not because he avoided failure, but because he learned how to rise after every fall. His journey taught him that strength is not about being perfect, but about being persistent.

This lesson helped Freed build resilience in his life. It gave him the courage to face challenges, learn from them, and keep moving forward. His story shows that true strength comes from growth, learning, and never giving up, even when life becomes difficult.

Accepting Setbacks as Hidden Steps Toward Success

Freed's journey became more challenging when he moved to a new city and joined a competitive firm where performance mattered more than effort. He worked under a senior manager named Victor, who believed only results define a person, and alongside colleagues like Marcus and Ethan, who were highly skilled and experienced. Freed felt pressure to prove himself, but soon he made a serious mistake in a client project that affected the team's outcome.

Victor did not hide his disappointment. He told Freed clearly that mistakes at this level could cost the company reputation. These words hit Freed hard and made him question his ability again.

Marcus, however, had a different approach. He shared his own past failures and explained how those setbacks shaped his growth. This gave Freed a new way to see his situation.

Instead of thinking that he had failed completely, Freed started seeing the setback as a moment of learning. He reviewed his work carefully and understood that his mistake came from lack of preparation and overconfidence. This realization was important because it gave him clarity on what needed to change.

Ethan, who was known for his discipline, advised Freed to slow down and focus on building strong fundamentals. He explained that success is not about avoiding mistakes, but about improving after them. Freed took this advice seriously and began working on his weak areas step by step.

With time, Freed started noticing a change in his thinking. Earlier, setbacks felt like an end, but now they felt like guidance. He stopped blaming situations and started taking responsibility for his actions. This shift made him mentally stronger and more focused.

Victor observed this change and gave Freed another opportunity to handle a smaller project. This time, Freed approached the work with patience and attention to detail. He did not rush or try to impress, but focused on doing things correctly.

The result was different. Freed completed the task successfully, not because it was easy, but because he had learned from his previous setback. This success gave him confidence, but more importantly, it gave him understanding.

Freed realized that setbacks are not failures, they are hidden steps that prepare a person for better results. They teach discipline, improve skills, and build mental strength. Without them, success would have no strong foundation.

This lesson became a core part of Freed's life. He no longer feared mistakes, because he understood their purpose. His journey showed that when a person accepts setbacks with the right mindset, they become powerful tools for growth and long-term success.

Learning from Failure Instead of Fearing It

Freed was still learning how to handle failure when he got a new chance to work on an important task with his team members Daniel, Oliver, and Jason. Daniel was strict but practical, Oliver was calm and experienced, and Jason was known for taking risks without fear. Freed wanted to perform well, but inside he was still afraid of making mistakes again. During the project, Freed made a wrong decision that slowed the team's progress. Instead of hiding it, Daniel asked him to explain what happened. Freed felt nervous, but he accepted his mistake honestly. Oliver then explained that failure is useful only when a person studies it, not when he fears it. Jason added that avoiding failure means avoiding growth. These words made Freed think deeply. He understood that his fear was stopping him from improving. After this, Freed started observing his mistakes carefully and learning from them without feeling ashamed. Slowly, his confidence improved because he knew he was growing with every experience. This change helped him become more active and less afraid of challenges.

Freed then created a simple habit of writing down what he learned after every mistake. This helped him see patterns in his thinking and actions. He noticed that most of his failures came from hesitation and lack of clarity. With this awareness, he started preparing better and taking clear decisions. Daniel later gave him another responsibility, and this time Freed handled it with a learning mindset instead of fear. His performance improved because he focused on progress, not perfection. He realized that failure is not a negative thing, but a guide that shows the right direction. This understanding made him mentally stronger and more open to new opportunities. Freed's journey showed that when a person stops fearing failure and starts learning from it, growth becomes faster and more meaningful.

Developing Emotional Control During Difficulties

After learning from his past mistakes in his job, Freed started feeling that he wanted more control over his life and growth. His earlier experiences with failure and pressure made him understand that working only for others was not helping him reach his full potential. During this time, he met new people like Nathan, Cole, and Victor, who were also thinking about starting something of their own. They shared similar struggles and a strong desire to grow. Freed decided to leave his job and join them to build a small business. In the beginning, everything was exciting, but soon they faced serious challenges like low sales and financial pressure. One big deal failed suddenly, and tension increased among them. Nathan became frustrated, Cole started doubting the decision, and Victor reacted emotionally. Freed also felt stressed, but he remembered his past lessons about staying calm. Instead of reacting, he controlled his emotions and focused on finding solutions. His calm behavior helped the team avoid conflict and think clearly. This showed him that emotional control is very important when situations are difficult.

As the business continued, problems did not stop, but Freed's mindset became stronger. He started taking time to think before speaking or acting. He understood that quick emotional reactions can damage both decisions and relationships. His previous job experience had already taught him how mistakes happen under pressure, so now he handled situations more wisely. Nathan slowly learned from Freed and became more patient, while Cole started trusting the process again. Their teamwork improved because Freed kept the environment stable. Over time, their business started growing slowly. Freed realized that leaving his job was a risk, but controlling emotions during difficult moments made that risk meaningful. His journey showed that success is not just about hard work, but also about staying balanced when things go wrong. This lesson helped him build both a strong business and a strong mindset.

Maintaining Hope in Challenging Situations

Freed's business journey became more difficult when his startup, a small digital marketing agency, started facing continuous losses. His partners Ethan, Lucas, and Ryan were already part of the team from the beginning, and they all had left their jobs with big expectations. Freed's family condition was still not strong, and he had responsibilities at home, which increased his pressure. When clients stopped renewing contracts and income became unstable, Ethan started worrying about finances, Lucas began losing confidence, and Ryan started thinking about quitting. In this situation, Freed also felt stress, but he understood that losing hope would break the entire team. Instead of focusing on problems, he kept reminding his team about their long-term vision and why they started this journey. He stayed positive in his words and actions, even when results were not coming immediately. This helped the team stay connected and not give up. Freed believed that difficult situations are temporary, but the mindset during those situations decides the future. Slowly, his positive attitude gave strength to others, and they continued working without losing direction.

Freed also took practical steps to improve their situation. He and his team started learning new marketing strategies, improving client communication, and offering better services at competitive prices. They reduced unnecessary expenses and focused only on important tasks. Freed made sure that even small achievements were appreciated, which helped maintain team morale. His hope was not blind belief, but a mix of patience and action. Over time, one small project turned into a stable client, and slowly their business started recovering. Freed realized that hope is not just about thinking positive, but about staying strong and taking action even when things are uncertain. His journey showed that a person who maintains hope during difficult times can survive challenges and eventually achieve success.

Adapting Quickly to Change

Freed's business started stabilizing, but the market suddenly changed when new digital trends and tools entered the industry. His agency began losing clients because their old methods were no longer effective. His teammates Mason, Tyler, and Jordan were confused and unsure about what to do next. Mason believed they should continue with the same strategy, Tyler felt they were falling behind, and Jordan was worried about losing more clients. Freed understood that this situation required quick adaptation, not fear or delay. Instead of resisting change, he decided to study the new trends and understand what the market really needed. He encouraged his team to learn new skills and accept that change is a part of growth. This mindset helped them move forward instead of staying stuck. Freed realized that success does not come from staying comfortable, but from adjusting quickly when situations change.

Freed and his team started updating their services by learning modern digital tools and improving their strategies. They attended online sessions, practiced new methods, and tested ideas on small projects. Slowly, their confidence returned as they started seeing better results. Tyler became more skilled, Mason accepted the need for change, and Jordan gained confidence again. Freed also improved his decision-making by staying flexible and open-minded. This helped the business grow again in a better way. Freed understood that adapting quickly is a powerful skill that helps a person survive and succeed in any situation. His journey showed that those who accept change and act fast always stay ahead, while those who resist it get left behind.

Turning Adversity into Opportunity

Freed reached a stage in his business where challenges were still coming, but his mindset had become stronger. Instead of waiting for perfect conditions, he started using every situation as a chance to improve. He focused on expanding his digital marketing business by learning advanced skills, improving service quality, and building better client relationships. Freed understood that growth comes when a person takes action during uncertain times. He worked on creating multiple income sources, improved his communication with clients, and built a clear system for delivering results. This helped him turn every small difficulty into a learning step. Slowly, his business started growing steadily because he was not stopping in difficult situations. He used his past experiences as strength and kept moving forward with confidence and clarity. Freed also started thinking long-term and made smart decisions to grow his business further. He invested time in understanding market needs and improved his strategies step by step. Instead of fearing challenges, he used them to make his work better and stronger. This approach helped him build a stable and successful business over time. Freed realized that opportunity is not something that comes easily, it is created by action and mindset. His journey shows that when a person focuses on growth and stays consistent, even difficult situations can become powerful turning points for success.

Building Confidence After Failure

Confidence does not come from always winning, it grows from how a person handles failure. When mistakes happen, instead of feeling weak, it is important to understand what went wrong and learn from it. This process helps in improving skills and making better decisions in the future. Small improvements after every failure slowly build strong self-belief. When a person keeps taking action even after setbacks, confidence starts increasing naturally. It is not about being perfect, but about being consistent and learning step by step. This mindset helps a person stay focused and move forward without fear.

Another important part of building confidence is trusting your own journey. Every person grows at a different pace, so comparing with others only creates doubt. Instead, focusing on personal progress makes the mind stronger and more stable. When a person starts noticing small wins and improvements, it creates a positive belief system. This belief helps in taking bigger decisions with clarity. Over time, confidence becomes a natural part of personality because it is built on real effort and experience. This teaches that failure is not a weakness, but a powerful tool that helps a person grow stronger and achieve long-term success.

Developing the Ability to Keep Going for the Long Term

Success in life does not come from short effort or quick results, it comes from the ability to stay consistent for a long period of time. Many people start their journey with high energy and motivation, but when results are slow or challenges come, they lose interest and stop. The real difference between successful and unsuccessful people is not talent, but the ability to continue when things become difficult. A person should understand that progress is always slow in the beginning, and results take time to appear. Instead of focusing on outcomes, it is better to focus on daily actions and habits. Small steps taken every day may look simple, but over time they create strong results. This mindset helps a person stay patient and committed without feeling frustrated. Long-term thinking builds mental strength and discipline, which are necessary for achieving any big goal in life.

Another important part of continuing for the long term is having clarity of purpose and strong inner motivation. When a person clearly understands why he is doing something, it becomes easier to stay focused even when the journey feels difficult. There will be times when results are not visible, and during such moments, many people start doubting themselves. But those who remind themselves of their purpose and keep moving forward become stronger with time. It is also important to accept that failures and delays are part of the process, not the end of it. A person should learn to adjust his methods, improve his approach, and keep working without stopping. Consistency with learning creates steady growth and builds confidence. Over time, this continuous effort creates a powerful habit of never giving up. This teaches that long-term success is not about doing something big once, but about doing small things daily with patience, focus, and determination until success becomes reality.

Learning Strength from People Who Never Gave Up

A person can gain strong life lessons by observing those who never give up in difficult situations. These individuals face many struggles, failures, and delays, but they continue their journey with patience and belief. Their life shows that real strength is not about avoiding problems, but about facing them with courage and moving forward step by step. When someone learns from such examples, he understands that success is not instant, but it is possible with steady effort. This learning builds inner motivation and helps in staying strong when situations become tough. It also develops a mindset of determination, which is important for long-term growth. Watching such journeys gives confidence that challenges can be handled with the right thinking and action. Another important lesson from such people is their ability to stay committed to their goals even when results are slow. They do not waste time blaming situations or others, instead they focus on improving themselves. This teaches that growth comes from effort, discipline, and learning from experience. A person should try to apply these lessons in daily life by staying regular in work and not stopping in the middle. It is also useful to read about real success stories, as they give clear understanding of how people achieve success over time. This approach builds mental strength and a strong attitude to continue the journey. In the long run, such thinking helps a person become stable, confident, and ready to face any challenge while moving ahead in life.

Awakening Inner Courage During Difficult Times

Freed's business journey reached a phase where challenges became more serious and constant. The market was competitive, growth was slow, and financial pressure was increasing day by day. At this stage, Freed realized that external situations cannot always be controlled, but inner strength can be developed. He started working on building courage from within by changing his thinking. Instead of feeling afraid of failure or loss, he began focusing on solutions and actions. He trained his mind to stay calm during stress and not take decisions based on fear. Freed understood that courage does not mean absence of fear, but it means taking action even when fear is present. He started facing problems one by one, without avoiding them, and this slowly made him mentally stronger. This habit helped him stay stable in situations where others might panic or give up. Over time, his decision-making improved, and he became more confident in handling uncertainty.

Freed also built his inner courage by creating strong daily habits and discipline in his work. He started planning his tasks clearly, improving his business strategies, and learning from every experience. Even when results were not immediate, he stayed consistent and trusted his process. He avoided negative thinking and focused only on what he could control. This approach helped him build a strong mindset that was not easily affected by challenges. As he continued taking steady action, his business started growing slowly but surely. Clients began trusting his work, and stability started coming into his business. Freed realized that courage grows when a person faces difficulties regularly and keeps moving forward with patience. His journey shows that inner courage is not something that comes instantly, it is built through repeated effort, learning, and belief in oneself. This strength helped him achieve success and also prepared him to handle future challenges with confidence and clarity.

Making Resilience a Natural Part of Your Personality

Resilience becomes powerful when it is not just used in difficult times but becomes a natural way of thinking and living. A person should train his mind to stay balanced in both good and bad situations. This means not getting too excited in success and not getting too low in failure. When someone starts accepting challenges as a normal part of life, his reactions become stronger and more controlled. This mindset helps in handling pressure without losing focus. Building such strength requires regular practice like staying calm, thinking clearly, and taking action without delay. Over time, this behavior becomes natural, and the person starts responding to problems with maturity and confidence. This kind of personality helps in long-term growth because it keeps a person stable and focused in every situation.

Another important part of developing this quality is creating strong habits that support mental strength. A person should focus on discipline, patience, and continuous improvement in daily life. Instead of reacting emotionally, he should learn to pause, understand the situation, and then respond wisely. This helps in making better decisions and avoiding unnecessary stress. It is also important to stay positive and learn from every experience, whether good or bad. When a person practices this regularly, resilience becomes a part of his nature. This inner strength helps him stay consistent, handle challenges easily, and move forward without fear. In the long run, such a personality becomes powerful, stable, and ready to face any situation while continuing the journey toward success.

11.

Mastering Time

Understanding that Time is Your Most Valuable Life Asset

Time is the most important resource in life because it controls every result a person gets in the future. Once a moment is gone, it never comes back, which makes it more valuable than money or any material thing. A person who understands this deeply starts becoming serious about how he spends each day. He stops delaying important work and avoids wasting time on activities that do not give any real benefit. Instead, he focuses on actions that improve his skills, knowledge, and overall growth. This thinking builds discipline and creates a strong daily routine. When time is used with purpose, even small efforts start giving meaningful results. Over time, this creates confidence because a person sees progress in his work and life. It also helps in building patience, because real success always takes time and continuous effort. Another important learning is that time should be used with planning and awareness, not in a random way. A person should divide his time carefully between work, learning, health, and rest so that life remains balanced. When time is managed properly, work becomes easier and stress reduces because tasks are completed on time. It also helps in making better decisions, as the mind stays clear and focused. A person who respects time starts choosing activities that give long-term benefits instead of short-term comfort. This builds self-control and improves focus in daily life. Over a long period, this habit shapes a strong and responsible personality. Such a person moves forward with clarity and uses every moment wisely to create growth, stability, and success in life

Realizing that Success Depends on How You Use Your Time

Success in life is not decided by luck or background, it is mainly decided by how a person uses his time every day. Every small action done daily builds the future, whether it is positive or negative. When a person starts understanding this, he becomes more careful about his daily routine and choices. Instead of spending time on unimportant things, he begins to focus on tasks that help him grow and move closer to his goals. This includes learning new skills, improving knowledge, and working with full focus. When time is used with clear purpose, even ordinary efforts start giving strong results over time. This thinking helps in building discipline and creates a habit of taking action regularly without delay. It also increases productivity because the person knows the value of every hour and uses it wisely.

Another important understanding is that proper use of time creates direction and clarity in life. A person who plans his day and sets priorities is able to complete more work with less stress. This helps in avoiding confusion and keeps the mind focused on what really matters. It also teaches the importance of consistency, because success is not achieved in one day but through repeated effort. When a person uses time carefully, he starts seeing improvement in his work, confidence, and results. Over a long period, this habit creates a strong foundation for success. A person who controls his time can control his life and create better opportunities through continuous effort

Choosing What Matters Most Every Single Day

Every day a person gets many choices, but only a few of them truly help in moving forward in life. When a person learns to focus on what really matters, his time and energy start giving better results.

Instead of doing random work, he begins to choose tasks that are directly connected to his goals. This creates clarity and direction, which is very important for growth. A person should start his day by deciding what is most important and complete that first. This habit helps in avoiding confusion and keeps the mind focused on meaningful work.

Another important step is understanding the difference between urgent and important tasks. Many things may look urgent, but they do not always help in long-term success. A person should give more attention to work that builds future results, like learning, planning, and improving skills. This thinking helps in using time wisely and prevents wasting energy on less useful activities. Over time, this builds a strong habit of making smart decisions daily.

It is also important to remove distractions that take away focus from important work. Small distractions like unnecessary phone use or random activities can reduce productivity. When a person becomes aware of this, he starts protecting his time and attention. This improves the quality of work and helps in completing tasks faster. Staying focused on important things daily builds strong discipline and control over actions.

Another valuable learning is that choosing what matters brings peace of mind. When a person knows he is working on the right things, he feels more confident and less stressed. It removes the pressure of doing too many tasks and creates a sense of balance. This also improves decision-making because the mind is not overloaded with unnecessary thoughts. A focused mind always performs better and gives better results.

Consistency in making the right choices is what creates real success. One good day is not enough, but repeated good decisions create strong progress. A person should practice this daily until it becomes a natural habit. Over time, this builds a powerful routine where important work becomes a priority without effort. This habit slowly transforms life in a positive direction.

In the long run, a person who always chooses what truly matters builds a strong and successful life. He becomes more productive, confident, and clear about his path. This approach helps in achieving goals step by step without confusion or delay. By focusing on what is important every day, a person creates steady growth and moves closer to success with clarity and purpose

Designing Your Day with Clear Purpose and Direction

A person who plans his day with clear purpose always moves faster toward his goals. When the day starts without a plan, time gets wasted in confusion and small unimportant tasks. But when there is clear direction, every action becomes meaningful and connected to growth. A simple habit like deciding tasks in advance can create a big difference in productivity. It helps the mind stay focused and reduces the chances of distraction. This approach builds discipline and gives a sense of control over daily life.

Having a clear structure for the day also helps in using energy in the right way. A person should place important work in the time when his mind is fresh and active. This improves the quality of work and saves time. Less important tasks can be done later without pressure. This balance makes the day more organized and reduces stress. Over time, this habit creates a strong routine that supports continuous progress.

Another useful practice is breaking the day into small sections with specific goals. Instead of thinking about the whole day, focusing on one part at a time makes work easier and more manageable. This method helps in completing tasks step by step without feeling overwhelmed. It also gives a sense of achievement after finishing each part, which keeps motivation high throughout the day.

Clear direction also helps in avoiding unnecessary decisions during the day. When tasks are already planned, the mind does not waste time thinking about what to do next. This saves mental energy and allows better focus on work. A person becomes more efficient because he spends more time on action rather than thinking. This improves overall performance and helps in achieving better results. It is also important to review the day and understand what was completed and what needs improvement. This reflection helps in making better plans for the next day. A person learns from his mistakes and improves his routine slowly. This process builds awareness and helps in using time more effectively in the future. In the long run, designing each day with clear purpose creates a strong foundation for success. It builds discipline, improves focus, and creates steady progress in life. A person who follows this habit moves ahead with clarity and confidence, making each day meaningful and productive

Using Deadlines as Tools to Increase Focus

Deadlines help a person stay serious about his work and avoid unnecessary delay. When there is no time limit, tasks often get postponed and energy gets wasted on unimportant things. But when a clear deadline is set, the mind becomes more alert and focused on completing the task on time. This creates a sense of urgency that pushes a person to take action without waiting for the perfect moment. It also improves time management because the person starts planning his work according to the available time. Over time, this habit builds discipline and makes work more organized and effective.

Another important benefit of deadlines is that they help in breaking large tasks into smaller and manageable parts. When a big task is given a final date, a person can divide it into steps and complete each step within a specific time. This makes the work less stressful and more clear. It also helps in tracking progress, as the person can see how much work is completed and what is left. This step-by-step approach increases confidence and keeps motivation strong throughout the process.

Deadlines also reduce distractions because the mind stays focused on finishing the work before the time limit. A person becomes more careful about how he spends each hour and avoids wasting time on activities that do not add value. This improves concentration and increases the quality of work. It also teaches responsibility, as the person understands the importance of completing tasks on time. Over time, this creates a strong habit of being reliable and consistent in work.

In the long run, using deadlines wisely helps a person become more productive and goal-oriented. It builds a sense of commitment and improves the ability to manage time under pressure. A person who follows deadlines regularly develops a focused mindset and achieves better results in less time

Creating Balance Between Work, Health, and Relationships

Trece understood that success is not only about earning money but also about living a stable and peaceful life. In the beginning, he was fully focused on work and ignored his health and family time, which slowly created stress and tiredness. After some time, he realized that without good health and strong relationships, success feels incomplete. He started giving equal importance to his daily routine by managing his work hours properly and fixing time for rest and family. This decision helped him feel more fresh, active, and mentally strong. He learned that balance is necessary to maintain long-term growth and happiness.

To improve his health, Trece added simple habits like regular exercise, proper sleep, and healthy eating in his daily routine. He understood that a healthy body supports a sharp and focused mind. At the same time, he made sure to spend quality time with his family without distractions. This strengthened his relationships and gave him emotional support. These changes helped him reduce stress and increased his overall productivity at work. He started feeling more stable and confident in handling both personal and professional life.

Trece also planned his work in a way that it did not affect his personal life. He avoided unnecessary overtime and focused on completing important tasks during fixed hours. This helped him create clear boundaries between work and personal time. As a result, he was able to give proper attention to both areas without feeling pressure. This balance made his life more organized and allowed him to enjoy his achievements without stress. It also improved his decision-making because his mind remained calm and clear.

In the long run, Trece's balanced approach helped him build a strong and fulfilling life. He became more productive at work, healthier in body, and happier in relationships. This balance gave him stability and peace, which are important for true success in life

Becoming Aware of Where Your Time is Actually Going

Most people think they are busy, but being busy does not always mean being productive. The real change starts when a person becomes aware of how his time is actually used during the day. When he observes his routine honestly, he may find that many hours are lost in small distractions, unplanned work, or activities that do not give any real value. This awareness is very powerful because it opens the truth about daily habits. Once a person understands where his time is going, he can start making better choices and use his time in a more meaningful way. It also helps in building self-discipline because the person becomes more conscious before spending time on anything.

A practical way to build this awareness is by noting down daily activities for a few days. This simple step shows a clear picture of time usage and helps in identifying areas of improvement. A person may realize that tasks take more time than expected or that too much time is spent on low-value work. This understanding helps in correcting mistakes and improving planning. It also builds responsibility, because the person starts taking control of his time instead of letting it pass without purpose. Over time, this habit leads to better time management and stronger focus.

Another important benefit is that awareness helps in reducing hidden time waste. Many small habits like checking the phone again and again or doing work without clear direction slowly consume a large part of the day. When a person becomes aware of these patterns, he can take simple steps to control them. This creates more free time for important tasks and improves productivity. It also increases mental clarity because the mind is not distracted by unnecessary activities. A focused mind works faster and gives better results.

In the long term, knowing how time is spent helps a person build a more organized and purposeful life. It improves decision-making, increases efficiency, and supports steady progress toward goals. A person who is aware of his time does not waste it without thinking and uses each day with intention and clarity

Building Daily Systems That Improve Productivity

A person becomes productive not by working randomly but by following a clear system every day. When work is done without a system, it creates confusion and wastes time in deciding what to do next. But when a simple daily system is followed, tasks become easier and more organized. A system can include fixed work hours, planned tasks, and a clear order of completing them. This reduces mental pressure and helps the person stay focused on important work. Over time, this habit creates consistency, which is the main key to long-term success.

Another important benefit of having a daily system is that it saves energy. When a person follows the same productive routine, he does not need to think again and again about what to do. This keeps the mind fresh and allows better focus on actual work. It also improves the speed and quality of work because the person becomes used to a structured way of working. Simple systems like starting the day with planning, working in focused time blocks, and taking short breaks can make a big difference in productivity.

Daily systems also help in tracking progress and improving

performance. When a person follows a system regularly, he can easily see what is working and what needs change. This helps in making small improvements in the routine. These small changes, when done consistently, create strong results over time. A system also builds discipline because it encourages action even on days when motivation is low. This makes productivity more stable and reliable.

In the long run, building a strong daily system helps a person achieve more with less stress. It creates balance, improves focus, and makes work more effective. A person who follows a system does not depend on mood or motivation but continues to move forward with consistency and control

Investing Time in Actions That Build Your Future

Every person has the same 24 hours, but the difference comes from how those hours are used. A wise person understands that time should not only be spent on daily work but also on actions that create a better future. This includes learning new skills, gaining knowledge, improving thinking, and working on long-term goals. When a person starts focusing on such activities, he begins to build a strong foundation for success. Instead of choosing short-term comfort, he chooses actions that may be difficult now but give better results later. This mindset helps in creating steady growth and meaningful progress in life.

Another important part is learning to invest time even when results are not immediate. Many valuable activities do not show quick results, but they slowly create strong improvement. A person who understands this continues his efforts with patience and consistency. This builds inner strength and discipline. It also increases confidence because the person knows he is working in the right direction. Over time, these efforts start showing results in the form of better opportunities, improved skills, and stronger decision-making ability.

It is also important to avoid activities that only give temporary satisfaction but do not add real value. A person should carefully choose where to spend his time and energy. By reducing time spent on low-value tasks, more time becomes available for meaningful work. This improves focus and helps in completing important tasks with better quality. It also creates a sense of purpose because every action is connected to future growth and success.

With continuous effort and smart use of time, a person slowly builds a life that is stable and successful. His daily actions become more powerful because they are aligned with his goals. This approach helps in creating better results, stronger confidence, and a clear path toward achieving long-term success

12.

The Power of Thoughts

Understanding that Every Action Begins with a Thought

Parker's life started changing when he realized that every action he takes first comes from a thought in his mind. Earlier, he used to act without thinking clearly, which often led to confusion and wrong decisions. But when he became aware of his thoughts, he understood that controlling his thinking can control his actions and results. He started observing his thoughts daily and tried to replace negative thinking with positive and clear ideas. This simple habit helped him make better decisions and take actions with confidence. Slowly, his daily actions became more focused and meaningful because they were guided by clear thinking.

Parker also learned that not all thoughts are useful, so he started choosing which thoughts to follow. Whenever a negative or doubtful thought came, he did not act on it immediately. Instead, he paused and replaced it with a better and more useful thought. This practice improved his mindset and helped him stay calm in difficult situations. As his thinking improved, his actions also became more planned and effective. He began to focus more on learning, improving skills, and working on his goals. This created a strong connection between his thoughts and actions, which helped him move forward in life.

Another important change was that Parker started using his thoughts to plan his day and future. He spent time thinking about what he wanted to achieve and how he could take steps toward it.

This made his actions more purposeful and reduced confusion. He stopped reacting to situations blindly and started responding with clear thinking. This improved his productivity and helped him use his time more wisely. His confidence also increased because he knew his actions were coming from strong and positive thinking. With regular practice, Parker built a habit of turning every useful thought into action. This made his progress steady and clear. His life became more organized, and he started achieving better results in his work and personal growth. By controlling his thoughts and turning them into meaningful actions, he created a strong path toward success and self-improvement

That Your Mindset Shapes Your Life Results

A person's mindset plays a very important role in deciding the direction of his life. The way a person thinks about himself, his work, and his future directly affects the actions he takes every day. If a person believes he can improve and grow, he starts taking steps to learn and move forward. But if he thinks negatively and doubts himself, he avoids action and misses opportunities. This shows that results are not only based on effort but also on the thinking behind that effort. A positive and growth-focused mindset helps a person stay motivated and take better decisions even in difficult situations. Another important point is that mindset affects how a person reacts to challenges. Some people see problems as obstacles, while others see them as chances to learn and improve. A strong mindset helps a person stay calm and think clearly instead of giving up. This improves problem-solving ability and builds confidence over time. When a person trains his mind to stay positive and focused, he becomes stronger from inside. This strength helps him handle pressure and continue working toward his goals without fear. Mindset also influences daily habits and routine. A person with a clear and positive mindset starts choosing actions that support his growth, like learning new skills, managing time properly, and staying disciplined. These small daily choices slowly create big changes in life. When thinking is clear, actions become more organized and results start improving. This creates a cycle where good thinking leads to good actions, and good actions lead to better results.

With continuous effort on improving mindset, a person can change his direction and build a better life. He becomes more confident, focused, and ready to take responsibility for his growth. This understanding helps him move forward with clarity and purpose, creating success through strong thinking and consistent action

Becoming Aware of Negative Thinking Patterns

Many people are not aware that their own thinking is holding them back. Negative thinking patterns like self-doubt, fear of failure, and overthinking slowly affect decisions and actions. When a person starts observing his thoughts carefully, he begins to notice these patterns. This awareness is very important because it helps in understanding what is going wrong inside the mind. Once a person identifies these negative thoughts, he gets the power to control them instead of being controlled by them. This creates a strong base for improving mindset and making better choices in life.

Another important step is accepting that negative thoughts are normal but they should not guide actions. A person should learn to pause and question his thoughts before believing them. For example, instead of thinking "I cannot do this," he can ask himself "What can I do to improve?" This small shift in thinking changes the direction of action. It helps in reducing fear and increases confidence. By doing this regularly, a person slowly weakens negative patterns and builds stronger, more positive thinking habits.

Awareness also helps in stopping automatic reactions. Many times, people react quickly based on negative thoughts without thinking clearly. But when a person becomes aware, he learns to respond with control and clarity. This improves decision-making and reduces mistakes. It also creates mental peace because the mind is

not filled with unnecessary negative thinking. A calm and clear mind helps in focusing on solutions instead of problems.
With regular practice, a person can train his mind to avoid negative thinking patterns and focus on better thoughts. This improves confidence, strengthens mindset, and helps in taking positive actions. By becoming aware and making small changes in thinking, a person can move toward growth, stability, and a more successful life

Replacing Limiting Thoughts with Empowering Ones

A person's growth depends a lot on the type of thoughts he allows in his mind. Limiting thoughts like "I am not good enough" or "I cannot succeed" slowly stop a person from taking action. The first step is to notice these thoughts and understand that they are not facts but only beliefs created over time. When a person becomes aware of this, he gets the chance to change his thinking. By replacing such thoughts with stronger and more positive ones, he starts building confidencc and clarity. This simple change in thinking can create a powerful impact on actions and results.
One useful method is to consciously change the language of thoughts. Instead of saying "I cannot do this," a person can think "I will learn how to do this." This shift creates hope and encourages action. Empowering thoughts do not ignore reality but focus on growth and improvement. They help a person stay motivated even when things are not easy. With regular practice, this habit starts becoming natural, and the mind begins to support progress instead of creating fear.
Another important benefit of changing thoughts is better emotional control. Negative thoughts often create stress and reduce confidence, while positive and strong thoughts bring calmness and stability. When the mind stays positive, decisions become clearer and actions become more effective. This also improves focus because the person is not distracted by doubt or fear. Over time, this creates a strong mindset that supports continuous growth and

success.

With consistent effort, replacing limiting thoughts with empowering ones becomes a powerful habit. It helps a person take better actions, build confidence, and move forward with clarity. This change in thinking creates a strong base for personal and professional success and helps in achieving meaningful goals with a positive mindset

Using Imagination to Create a Clear Vision of Success

Imagination is a powerful tool that helps a person see what is not yet real but possible in the future. When a person uses imagination in the right way, he can create a clear picture of his goals and success. This clear vision gives direction and purpose to daily actions. Without a clear image in the mind, a person may feel confused and lost. But when he imagines his success in detail, like the kind of work he wants, the life he wants to live, and the person he wants to become, it becomes easier to take focused steps. This habit builds clarity and helps in making better decisions every day.

Another important benefit of imagination is that it increases motivation. When a person regularly thinks about his future success, he feels more connected to his goals. This connection creates excitement and pushes him to take action even when things are not easy. It also reduces fear because the mind starts focusing on positive outcomes instead of negative possibilities. By visualizing success, a person prepares his mind to believe that achieving goals is possible. This belief becomes a strong force that supports continuous effort and improvement.

Imagination also helps in planning and problem solving. When a person clearly sees his future, he can think about the steps required to reach there. This makes actions more organized and reduces confusion. He can also imagine possible challenges and prepare solutions in advance. This improves confidence and reduces mistakes. A clear vision acts like a guide that keeps a person on the right path and prevents him from getting distracted by unimportant

things.
With regular use of imagination, a person builds a strong and clear vision of success. This vision guides his thoughts, actions, and decisions in the right direction. It helps him stay focused, motivated, and confident while working toward his goals and creating a meaningful and successful life

Building Beliefs That Support Your Growth

Beliefs are like the base on which a person builds his life. If a person believes that he can learn, improve, and achieve his goals, he naturally starts taking actions in that direction. But if he believes that success is not possible for him, he stops trying before even starting. This shows that beliefs directly affect actions and results. A person should carefully check what he believes about himself, his abilities, and his future. By choosing strong and positive beliefs, he can create a mindset that supports growth and progress.
Strong beliefs are not created in one day, they are built slowly through learning and experience. When a person starts learning new skills, gaining knowledge, and achieving small wins, his confidence increases. These small successes help in changing old limiting beliefs into stronger ones. It is also important to surround yourself with positive information, good ideas, and inspiring examples. This helps the mind accept new possibilities and build beliefs that encourage growth instead of stopping it.
Another important point is that beliefs should be supported by action. Only thinking positive is not enough, a person must take steps that match his beliefs. When actions and beliefs work together, results start improving. This also creates trust in oneself because the person can see his progress clearly. Over time, this habit builds a strong mindset that is ready to face challenges and continue moving forward without fear or doubt.
With continuous effort, a person can replace weak beliefs with powerful ones that support his journey. This change helps in

building confidence, improving decisions, and taking consistent action toward goals. A strong belief system acts as inner support and helps a person grow, achieve success, and create a meaningful and purposeful life

Training Your Subconscious Mind for Positive Outcomes

The subconscious mind works silently in the background and controls many habits, reactions, and decisions without a person even realizing it. Whatever thoughts a person repeats again and again slowly become part of this deeper mind. If negative thoughts are repeated, the subconscious starts accepting them as truth and shapes actions in that direction. That is why it becomes very important to feed the mind with positive, clear, and growth-focused thoughts. When a person becomes aware of this process, he can start guiding his mind in a better way and create positive outcomes in life.

One effective way to train the subconscious mind is through repetition and consistency. When a person regularly thinks about his goals, speaks positive statements, and imagines success, the mind starts accepting these ideas as reality. This builds confidence and reduces fear. Over time, actions start aligning with these thoughts without much effort. This makes it easier to stay focused and take the right steps even in difficult situations. Consistent positive input helps the mind stay strong and stable.

Another important method is controlling the information that enters the mind. What a person reads, watches, and listens to directly affects thinking patterns. By choosing useful and inspiring content, a person can shape his subconscious in a positive way. It is also helpful to avoid negative environments that create doubt or fear. A clean and positive mental environment supports better thinking and helps in building a strong inner mindset that encourages growth and improvement.

With regular practice, the subconscious mind becomes a powerful support system that works in favor of success. It helps in making better decisions, staying calm under pressure, and taking confident actions. This inner strength allows a person to move forward with clarity and purpose, creating positive results and steady progress in life

Developing a Habit of Positive Thinking in Daily Life

A middle class man often faces pressure of responsibilities, limited resources, and uncertain future, but his thinking can decide how he handles these situations. When he starts building a habit of positive thinking, he slowly changes the way he sees problems and opportunities. Instead of focusing on what is missing, he begins to focus on what can be improved. This shift in thinking helps him stay calm and take better decisions even in difficult situations. Positive thinking does not mean ignoring reality, it means choosing a better response to every situation. This habit helps him move forward step by step with confidence and hope.

In daily life, this man starts practicing simple habits like thinking about solutions instead of problems, appreciating small progress, and believing that effort will bring results. These small changes create a big difference in his mindset. He stops comparing his life with others and starts focusing on his own growth. This improves his mental peace and helps him stay focused on his goals. Slowly, his actions become more consistent and meaningful, which improves his financial condition and overall life stability.

As time passes, his positive thinking starts showing clear results in his future. He becomes more confident in taking decisions, starts learning new skills, and finds better opportunities. His family also feels more secure because of his stable mindset and actions. His children learn from his behavior and develop a strong mindset from an early age. This creates a positive environment at home where growth and improvement become a natural part of life. His journey shows that a strong mindset can change not only one person's life but also the future of the entire family.

With continuous effort, this habit becomes a natural part of his personality. His thinking stays focused on growth, his actions stay consistent, and his life moves in a positive direction. This simple but powerful change helps him build a better future, achieve stability, and create a life filled with purpose and progress

Practicing Gratitude to Shift Your Mindset

Gratitude is a simple habit but it has a deep impact on the way a person thinks and feels. When a person starts focusing on what he already has instead of what is missing, his mindset begins to change in a positive way. This shift helps in reducing stress, comparison, and negative thinking. A person who practices gratitude regularly feels more satisfied and calm because he learns to value small things in life. This creates mental peace and allows him to think more clearly about his goals and actions.

One important benefit of gratitude is that it improves emotional strength. When a person faces challenges, gratitude helps him stay balanced instead of feeling frustrated. He starts noticing that even in difficult situations, there are still things to learn and appreciate. This mindset builds inner stability and prevents negative thoughts from taking control. It also helps in maintaining motivation because the person does not feel completely lost or hopeless.

Gratitude also improves relationships and daily interactions. When a person appreciates others and expresses thankfulness, it creates stronger connections and a positive environment. This not only improves personal life but also supports growth in professional areas. People feel more comfortable and supportive around someone who values and respects them. This positive environment helps a person stay focused and motivated in his journey.

With regular practice, gratitude becomes a natural way of thinking. It shifts the mind toward positivity, improves emotional balance, and supports better decision making. This habit helps a person move forward with clarity, build stronger relationships, and create a more peaceful and successful life

Staying Mentally Strong During Difficult Situations

Difficult situations are a part of every person's life, but the way a person handles them decides his growth and future. Mental strength helps a person stay calm and think clearly when problems arise. Instead of reacting with fear or panic, a strong mind focuses on finding solutions. This ability does not come automatically, it is built by practicing control over thoughts and emotions. When a person trains himself to stay steady in tough times, he becomes more confident in facing any situation.

One important way to stay mentally strong is to accept reality without overthinking. Many people waste energy by worrying too much about problems instead of taking action. A strong mindset helps a person focus on what can be done instead of what cannot be changed. This improves decision making and reduces stress. It also helps in saving time and energy, which can be used in productive work. By staying focused on solutions, a person can move forward even in challenging conditions.

Mental strength also grows when a person learns from difficult experiences. Every challenge teaches something valuable if a person is ready to understand it. Instead of feeling defeated, he starts seeing problems as learning opportunities. This builds inner confidence and prepares him for future challenges. Over time, he becomes more stable and less affected by negative situations. This stability helps him stay consistent in his efforts and maintain progress in life.

With regular practice, a person develops the ability to stay strong in any situation. His thinking becomes clear, his actions become controlled, and his confidence increases. This strength helps him face challenges with courage, take better decisions, and continue moving toward his goals with focus and determination

Strengthening Your Mind to Handle Pressure

Pressure is a part of life, especially when a person is trying to grow and achieve something meaningful. A strong mind helps a person stay calm and think clearly even when situations become stressful. Instead of feeling overwhelmed, he learns to focus on what he can control. This shift in thinking reduces unnecessary stress and improves decision making. When a person trains his mind to stay steady during pressure, he becomes more confident in handling responsibilities and challenges. This ability helps him perform better and move forward without fear.

One important way to build mental strength is by practicing control over thoughts and reactions. Many times, pressure increases because of overthinking and negative imagination. A person should learn to pause, take a breath, and focus on solutions instead of problems. This simple habit brings clarity and helps in taking the right actions. It also improves emotional control, which is very important during difficult situations. By staying focused and calm, a person can handle pressure in a more effective way.

Another powerful method is preparing the mind before facing challenges. When a person expects difficulties and trains himself to stay strong, pressure does not feel shocking or unbearable. He starts seeing challenges as part of growth instead of obstacles. This mindset reduces fear and increases confidence. Regular habits like discipline, planning, and self-control also support mental strength. These habits create stability and help a person stay balanced even when situations are not easy.

With continuous practice, a person develops a strong and stable mindset that can handle pressure without losing focus. His thinking becomes clear, his actions become controlled, and his confidence grows. This inner strength allows him to face any situation with courage and move forward with determination toward his goals

Using Self-Talk to Guide Your Actions

Self-talk is the voice inside the mind that continuously guides thoughts, decisions, and actions. Many people are not aware of it, but this inner conversation plays a very important role in shaping behavior. When a person speaks negatively to himself, he starts doubting his abilities and avoids taking action. But when he uses positive and clear self-talk, it builds confidence and creates a strong mindset. This simple habit helps a person stay focused and make better choices in daily life.

A person can improve his self-talk by becoming aware of his thoughts and slowly replacing negative statements with positive and practical ones. For example, instead of saying "I cannot do this," he can say "I will learn and improve step by step." This small change creates a big difference in thinking and action. Positive self-talk does not mean ignoring reality, it means guiding the mind toward solutions and progress. This approach helps in reducing fear and increasing confidence while working toward goals.

Self-talk also helps during difficult situations when a person feels confused or stressed. In such moments, the right inner words can bring clarity and control. By reminding himself to stay calm, focus on solutions, and keep moving forward, a person can manage pressure more effectively. This habit improves emotional control and keeps the mind stable. It also helps in maintaining consistency because the person continues guiding himself in the right direction. With regular practice, self-talk becomes a powerful tool that supports growth and success. It helps in building confidence, improving decisions, and taking consistent action. A strong and positive inner voice acts like a guide that keeps a person focused, motivated, and moving forward toward a meaningful and successful life

13.

Opportunity in Obstacles

Seeing Every Challenge as a Chance to Grow Stronger

Challenges are a natural part of life, but the way a person sees them decides his growth. When a person starts seeing challenges as chances to become stronger, his mindset begins to change. Instead of feeling afraid or avoiding problems, he becomes more open to facing them. This attitude helps him learn new skills, improve his thinking, and develop confidence. Every difficult situation carries a lesson, and when a person focuses on learning instead of complaining, he starts growing in a powerful way.

One important benefit of this mindset is that it reduces fear and builds courage. When a person accepts that challenges are part of progress, he stops expecting an easy path. This prepares his mind for reality and helps him stay calm during tough situations. He begins to understand that growth happens outside the comfort zone. By facing challenges again and again, he trains his mind to handle pressure and uncertainty without losing focus.

This approach also improves problem-solving ability. When a person treats challenges as opportunities, he starts thinking about solutions instead of worrying about problems. This improves his decision making and helps him take better actions. He becomes more creative and flexible in his thinking. Over time, he develops a strong mindset that is not easily affected by negative situations. This strength helps him move forward even when conditions are not in his favor.

With continuous effort, this way of thinking becomes a natural part of personality. A person becomes stronger, more confident, and more focused on growth. He starts using every challenge as a stepping stone to improve himself and move closer to his goals. This mindset helps him build a successful and meaningful life with strength and determination

Changing Your View from Problem to Possibility

Many people get stuck in life because they only focus on problems, not on what can be done. When a person changes his view from problem to possibility, his thinking becomes more powerful and solution-focused. Instead of asking "why is this happening," he starts asking "what can I do now." This simple shift in thinking opens new ways and ideas that were not visible before. It helps a person stay positive and active instead of feeling stuck or helpless. This mindset creates energy to move forward and take action.

One important advantage of this approach is that it reduces stress and overthinking. When a person keeps thinking about problems, his mind becomes heavy and confused. But when he starts focusing on possibilities, his mind becomes lighter and more creative. He begins to explore different options and find better ways to handle the situation. This improves his confidence because he sees that every situation has some solution if he looks at it with the right mindset.

This way of thinking also builds strong decision-making skills. A person who looks for possibilities becomes more flexible and open to change. He does not get stuck in one way of thinking but keeps adjusting according to the situation. This helps him take better decisions and move ahead even in uncertain conditions. Over time, he develops a mindset that naturally looks for growth, improvement, and new opportunities in every situation.

With regular practice, this habit becomes part of daily thinking. A person starts seeing opportunities where others see problems. His confidence grows, his actions become more effective, and his progress becomes steady. This powerful mindset helps him face challenges with clarity and move toward success with a positive and focused approach

Finding Valuable Lessons Inside Failures

Failure is often seen as something negative, but in reality, it carries valuable lessons that can help a person grow. When a person changes his thinking and starts looking for learning inside failure, he becomes stronger and wiser. Instead of feeling disappointed, he begins to analyze what went wrong and how it can be improved. This mindset helps him turn mistakes into guidance for better actions. Every failure then becomes a step that moves him closer to success.

One important benefit of this approach is that it removes fear of trying new things. When a person understands that failure is not the end but a learning process, he becomes more confident in taking risks. He stops worrying about what others will think and focuses more on improving himself. This builds courage and helps him step out of his comfort zone. As a result, he gains more experience and develops skills that are necessary for growth.

This habit also improves decision-making and awareness. When a person learns from past failures, he becomes more careful and thoughtful in his future actions. He starts avoiding the same mistakes and makes better choices. This improves his ability to handle situations in a smarter way. Over time, he builds a strong mindset that does not break under pressure but learns and adapts continuously.

With regular reflection and learning, failure becomes a powerful teacher instead of a barrier. A person grows mentally, becomes more confident, and moves forward with clarity. This way of thinking helps him improve consistently and build a successful and meaningful life through learning and persistence

Thinking Creatively to Solve Difficult Situations

Difficult situations require more than normal thinking, they require a creative approach. When a person learns to think creatively, he starts looking at problems from different angles instead of following the same old methods. This helps him find solutions that are simple, practical, and effective. Creative thinking is not about being perfect, it is about being open to new ideas and trying different ways until something works. This mindset helps a person stay flexible and active even when situations are confusing or challenging.

One important benefit of creative thinking is that it breaks mental limitations. Many times, people feel stuck because they believe there is only one way to solve a problem. But when a person trains his mind to explore new possibilities, he begins to see multiple options. This increases his confidence and reduces stress because he knows there is always a way forward. It also helps him stay calm and focused instead of feeling frustrated or helpless.

Creative thinking also improves decision making and problem-solving skills. When a person uses imagination along with logic, he is able to come up with better and smarter solutions. He learns to adapt quickly and handle unexpected situations with ease. This skill becomes very useful in both personal and professional life. Over time, he becomes more independent because he can handle challenges without depending too much on others.

With regular practice, creative thinking becomes a natural habit. A person starts finding solutions quickly, stays positive in tough situations, and continues to move forward without fear. This ability helps him grow continuously and build a strong, confident, and successful life by handling every challenge in a smart and effective way

Accepting Mistakes as Part of Progress

Hekter started his journey in the cloth industry with big dreams but very little experience. In the beginning, he made many wrong decisions like choosing poor quality fabric, trusting the wrong suppliers, and not understanding customer needs. These mistakes caused heavy losses and stress in his life. For some time, he felt disappointed and even thought of quitting. But instead of blaming others or feeling stuck, he made a strong decision to accept his mistakes honestly. He understood that mistakes are not failure, they are lessons that show the right path if a person is ready to learn.

After accepting his past errors, Hekter began to carefully study where he went wrong. He improved his knowledge about fabric quality, market demand, and customer preferences. He started taking small and careful steps instead of rushing decisions. He also learned to verify people before trusting them in business. This change in thinking made him more aware and responsible. Slowly, his confidence started growing because now his actions were based on learning, not guesswork.

With this new mindset, his business started improving step by step. He focused on providing better quality products and building trust with customers. Even when small problems came, he did not panic because he had already learned how to handle mistakes. His past experiences became his strength. He became more patient, disciplined, and focused on long-term growth instead of quick success. This helped him build a stable and growing business.

Over time, Hekter transformed his failures into success by accepting mistakes as part of progress. His journey shows that no one becomes successful without facing errors. The difference is that successful people learn, improve, and move forward without losing hope. This mindset helps a person grow stronger, wiser, and more confident, and it leads him toward a successful and meaningful life

Staying Flexible When Situations Change

Life and work do not always go according to plan, and this is where flexibility becomes a powerful strength. A person who stays flexible is able to adjust his thinking and actions according to changing situations instead of feeling stuck or frustrated. This quality helps him stay calm and open-minded when things do not happen as expected. Instead of resisting change, he accepts it and looks for new ways to move forward. This mindset reduces stress and allows him to handle uncertainty with confidence and clarity.

One important benefit of flexibility is that it helps a person adapt quickly without losing focus on his goals. When plans fail or situations shift, he does not waste time complaining. He immediately looks for alternative solutions and takes action. This saves time and energy, and it keeps progress moving. Flexible thinking also improves creativity because a person starts exploring new ideas and approaches instead of depending on one fixed method. This makes him stronger in handling different types of challenges.

Flexibility also plays a major role in decision making. A rigid mindset often leads to wrong decisions because it does not consider changing conditions. But a flexible person observes the situation carefully and adjusts his choices based on what is practical. This improves results and reduces mistakes. It also helps in building better relationships because such a person is more understanding and willing to adjust when needed. This balance creates stability in both personal and professional life.

With regular practice, flexibility becomes a natural habit that supports growth and success. A person becomes more confident in handling change, more creative in solving problems, and more focused on moving forward. This ability allows him to face any situation with a positive attitude and continue progressing toward his goals with strength and clarity

Turning Setbacks into New Starting Points

Setbacks are not the end of the journey, they are signals that something needs to be improved or changed. When a person learns to see setbacks as new starting points, his mindset becomes stronger and more positive. Instead of feeling stuck or disappointed, he begins to look for what can be done next. This thinking helps him stay active and focused on progress. Every setback carries a lesson, and when a person uses that lesson wisely, he turns a negative situation into a new opportunity for growth.

One important benefit of this approach is that it builds resilience and courage. A person who accepts setbacks does not fear failure because he knows he can start again with better understanding. This removes pressure and allows him to take bold steps without hesitation. He becomes more confident in his ability to handle difficulties. This mindset also helps him stay patient, because he understands that success is a process that includes ups and downs.

This way of thinking also improves planning and decision making. After facing a setback, a person becomes more aware of his mistakes and weaknesses. He starts making better plans and takes more thoughtful actions. This reduces the chances of repeating the same errors. He also becomes more focused on improvement instead of perfection. This helps him grow steadily and build a strong foundation for future success.

With continuous effort, setbacks lose their negative impact and become part of the growth journey. A person becomes stronger, more focused, and more determined to move forward. He learns to restart with clarity and confidence every time he faces difficulty. This powerful mindset helps him create new opportunities and move closer to his goals with strength and persistence

Keeping Your Drive Alive During Hard Times

Hard times are part of every journey, but what makes a difference is how a person keeps his drive alive during those moments. When situations become difficult, many people lose motivation and stop taking action. But a strong person understands that difficult phases are temporary and continues moving forward with patience and focus. He reminds himself why he started and what he wants to achieve. This inner drive becomes the force that keeps him going even when results are not visible.

One important way to maintain this drive is by focusing on small progress instead of expecting big results quickly. When a person breaks his goals into small steps, he feels a sense of achievement regularly. This keeps his energy positive and prevents frustration. He learns to appreciate effort and consistency rather than only final success. This mindset helps him stay motivated and continue working even when the journey feels slow or challenging.

Another key factor is controlling negative thoughts during tough times. When a person allows doubt and fear to take control, his drive becomes weak. But when he trains his mind to stay positive and solution-focused, he becomes mentally strong. He starts seeing difficulties as temporary situations that can be handled with effort and patience. This mental strength helps him stay stable and take consistent action without losing direction.

With continuous effort and belief, a person builds a powerful habit of staying driven even in hard times. His focus becomes strong, his actions remain consistent, and his confidence keeps growing. This ability helps him move forward without giving up and brings him closer to his goals with determination and inner strength

Building Strong Character Through Struggle

Struggle is not just a difficult phase, it is a powerful process that shapes a person's character. When a person goes through tough situations, he learns patience, discipline, and emotional control. These qualities cannot be learned in comfort. Instead of avoiding struggle, a wise person accepts it as a part of growth. This mindset helps him stay strong and focused even when life becomes challenging. Struggles teach lessons that make a person more mature and responsible in his actions.

One important benefit of facing struggle is that it builds inner strength. When a person handles problems again and again, his mind becomes more stable and confident. He learns how to control his reactions and think clearly in difficult situations. This makes him less dependent on others and more capable of handling life on his own. Over time, he develops courage that helps him face bigger challenges without fear or hesitation.

Struggle also improves decision making and understanding of life. A person who has faced difficulties becomes more aware of his choices. He learns to value effort, time, and opportunities. This awareness helps him make better decisions and avoid unnecessary mistakes. He becomes more focused on what truly matters and stops wasting energy on things that do not support his growth. This clarity plays an important role in building a strong and stable life.

With continuous effort and learning, struggle becomes a foundation for strong character. A person becomes disciplined, confident, and mentally strong. His thinking becomes practical, his actions become meaningful, and his direction becomes clear. This strength helps him move forward with determination and build a successful and respectful life through experience and growth

Learning Patience and Persistence Through Challenges

Challenges are powerful teachers that help a person develop patience and persistence, which are very important for long-term success. When things do not happen quickly, many people feel frustrated and give up. But a strong person understands that meaningful progress takes time and effort. He learns to stay calm and continue working even when results are not immediate. This ability to wait and keep going builds inner strength and helps him stay focused on his goals without losing hope.

Patience helps a person control emotions and avoid making rushed decisions. When facing difficulties, instead of reacting quickly, he takes time to think and understand the situation. This improves his ability to handle problems wisely. At the same time, persistence keeps him moving forward step by step. Even when the path becomes difficult, he does not stop. He continues his efforts with discipline and belief, knowing that consistent action brings results

over time.
This combination of patience and persistence also improves confidence and self-trust. When a person keeps working despite challenges, he starts believing in his ability to overcome difficulties. Every small progress strengthens his mindset and makes him more determined. He learns that success is not about speed but about consistency and effort. This understanding helps him stay committed and avoid distractions that can slow down his journey.
With regular practice, patience and persistence become natural qualities that support growth and success. A person becomes more stable, focused, and determined in his actions. He handles challenges with a calm mind and continues moving forward without giving up. This strong mindset helps him achieve his goals and build a successful and meaningful life through steady effort and dedication

Converting Every Obstacle into a New Opportunity

Dukon started his journey with big dreams but faced many obstacles in the early stage of his career. He wanted to build his own business, but he did not have enough money, proper guidance, or strong connections. Many times his plans failed, and he faced rejection from people he trusted. Instead of giving up, Dukon decided to change his thinking. He stopped seeing obstacles as barriers and started looking at them as chances to learn something new. This shift in mindset helped him stay strong and continue moving forward even when situations were difficult.
When Dukon faced problems like lack of funds, he used it as an opportunity to learn financial management and started working with small resources. When people rejected his ideas, he improved his communication and presentation skills. Every obstacle pushed him to develop a new skill or improve his thinking. He did not waste time complaining, instead he focused on finding solutions. This habit made him more creative and practical. Slowly, he began

to understand that obstacles were actually guiding him toward better decisions and stronger growth.

As time passed, Dukon's confidence increased because he had learned how to handle difficult situations. He started making better plans and avoided repeating past mistakes. His mindset became focused on growth and opportunity. Even when new challenges came, he remained calm and looked for what he could gain from the situation. This attitude helped him move ahead steadily and build a strong foundation for his work. People around him also started respecting his ability to stay positive and solution-oriented. Dukon's journey shows that obstacles are not the end, they are new beginnings in disguise. When a person learns to convert every difficulty into an opportunity, he becomes stronger, smarter, and more confident. This mindset helps him grow continuously and move closer to success with clarity and determination. It teaches that real progress comes from learning, adapting, and taking action even when the path is not easy

14.

Purpose Driven Life

Discovering a Deeper Purpose That Gives True Meaning and Direction to Your Life Journey

Every person wants success, but real satisfaction comes when life has a clear purpose. When a person starts discovering a deeper purpose, his thinking changes from just earning or surviving to living with meaning. He begins to ask important questions like what truly matters, what kind of life he wants to build, and how he can make a difference. This self-awareness helps him understand his values and priorities. It gives him a clear direction so that his efforts are not wasted on things that do not bring real growth or happiness.

When a person connects with his purpose, his actions become more focused and meaningful. He stops following others blindly and starts making decisions based on what truly matters to him. This helps him stay consistent even when situations are difficult. His motivation becomes stronger because now he is not just working for short-term results, but for something bigger and meaningful. This clarity reduces confusion and helps him move forward with confidence and determination.

A deeper purpose also gives emotional strength during tough times. When challenges come, a person with purpose does not give up easily because he knows why he started. This strong reason keeps him going even when progress is slow. He learns to stay patient and committed because his vision is clear. This mindset helps him handle pressure, avoid distractions, and stay focused on his journey without losing direction.

With time, living with purpose creates a meaningful and fulfilling life. A person feels satisfied not just because of achievements, but because his actions align with his values and goals. He builds a life that has clarity, direction, and impact. This approach helps him grow continuously and create a journey that is not only successful but also deeply meaningful and satisfying

Identifying What Truly Excites Your Heart and Naturally Drives Your Actions

Every person has something inside that naturally excites him, but many people ignore it because of fear, pressure, or confusion. When a person starts identifying what truly excites his heart, he begins to understand himself better. This excitement is not just temporary happiness, it is something that gives energy, interest, and a strong desire to take action. It can be any work, skill, or goal that makes him feel alive and motivated without force. Recognizing this inner drive helps him choose the right path instead of following what others expect.

When a person works on something that truly interests him, his actions become natural and consistent. He does not need external pressure to stay focused because his interest itself becomes the motivation. This improves his performance and helps him learn faster. He becomes more creative, more engaged, and more dedicated to his work. This type of connection between interest and action makes the journey enjoyable and less stressful. It also helps him stay committed even when challenges come.

Identifying this inner excitement also helps in making better life decisions. A person becomes clear about what he wants and what he should avoid. He stops wasting time on things that do not match his interests or values. This clarity saves energy and helps him focus on meaningful work. It also builds confidence because he knows he is moving in the right direction based on his true self, not based on others' opinions.

With time, following what truly excites the heart creates a strong and fulfilling life. A person feels satisfied because his actions are connected with his inner passion and purpose. He grows continuously, stays motivated, and builds a life that feels meaningful and rewarding. This understanding helps him take clear steps and move forward with confidence and direction

Aligning Your Daily Goals with Your Core Values to Live with Honesty and Clarity

Every person has certain values like honesty, respect, growth, and responsibility, but many times daily actions do not match these values. When a person starts aligning his daily goals with his core values, his life becomes more clear and meaningful. He begins to take actions that truly represent who he is and what he believes in. This removes confusion and inner conflict because his decisions are now based on strong principles. It helps him stay true to himself instead of getting influenced by outside pressure.

When goals are connected with values, consistency becomes easier. A person does not feel forced to work because his actions are connected with his beliefs. This creates natural discipline and focus. For example, if growth is an important value, he will automatically choose tasks that improve his knowledge and skills. This type of clarity helps him use his time wisely and avoid distractions that do not support his purpose. It also builds strong confidence because he knows he is moving in the right direction.

This approach also improves decision making in daily life. When a person faces difficult choices, his values act like a guide. He does not feel confused because he knows what is right for him. This helps him avoid wrong paths and unnecessary mistakes. It also builds trust with others because his actions are honest and consistent. People respect a person who lives with clear values and strong principles. This creates better relationships and a positive image in both personal and professional life.

With regular practice, living with aligned goals and values creates a stable and fulfilling life. A person feels peaceful and confident because there is no gap between what he thinks and what he does. His direction becomes clear, his actions become meaningful, and his life becomes more focused. This strong connection between values and goals helps him grow continuously and build a life based on honesty, clarity, and purpose

Choosing Intentional Living Instead of Drifting Without Direction or Purpose

Many people live their life without clear direction, just following daily routine without thinking about where they are going. This creates confusion, stress, and lack of satisfaction. When a person chooses intentional living, he starts making conscious decisions about how he spends his time, energy, and effort. He becomes aware of his actions and ensures that every step is connected to his goals and values. This brings clarity in life and helps him avoid wasting time on things that do not add real value.

Intentional living helps a person take control of his life instead of depending on situations. He plans his day with purpose and focuses on what truly matters. Instead of reacting to everything, he learns to respond wisely. This improves productivity and helps him stay disciplined. When actions are planned with intention, results also become more meaningful. He starts seeing progress because his efforts are directed in the right way.

This way of living also improves mental peace and confidence. When a person knows why he is doing something, he feels more stable and focused. He does not get easily distracted or influenced by others. His decisions become stronger because they are based on clear thinking. This helps him avoid confusion and regret. He becomes more responsible for his actions and learns to handle situations with maturity and balance.

With regular practice, intentional living becomes a natural habit. A person becomes more aware, focused, and clear about his journey. His actions start creating real impact, and his life moves in a meaningful direction. This approach helps him build a life with purpose, clarity, and strong control over his choices and future

Creating a Positive Impact That Adds Value to Other People's Lives

A meaningful life is not only about personal success, it is also about how much value a person adds to others. When a person focuses on creating a positive impact, his thinking shifts from self-centered goals to contribution and service. He starts asking how his actions can help, support, or improve someone else's life. This mindset builds a deeper sense of purpose and satisfaction. It also creates strong emotional connection because helping others brings inner happiness that material success alone cannot give.

When a person adds value to others, he naturally builds trust and respect. People feel comfortable and confident around someone who genuinely wants to help. This improves relationships in both personal and professional life. It also opens new opportunities because people prefer to work and connect with those who are supportive and reliable. By sharing knowledge, offering help, or solving problems, a person becomes valuable in the eyes of others. This value creates long-lasting impact and recognition.

This approach also improves personal growth and understanding. When a person helps others, he learns new perspectives and experiences. It makes him more patient, kind, and emotionally strong. He starts understanding people better and becomes more aware of real-life challenges. This awareness improves his thinking and decision making. It also helps him grow as a responsible and mature individual who is not only focused on himself but also on the well-being of others.

With consistent effort, creating positive impact becomes a natural part of life. A person feels fulfilled because his actions are meaningful and useful for others. His life gains purpose, respect, and strong connections. This mindset helps him build a balanced and successful life where growth is not only personal but also shared with others through value and contribution

Understanding That Real Fulfillment Comes from Growth, Contribution, and Inner Satisfaction

Many people think success means only money, status, or external achievements, but true fulfillment comes from deeper things like personal growth, helping others, and feeling satisfied from within. When a person understands this, his priorities start changing. He begins to focus on improving himself, learning new skills, and becoming a better version of who he is. This growth gives him confidence and a sense of progress, which brings real happiness that cannot be taken away easily.

Contribution also plays a very important role in fulfillment. When a person uses his knowledge, time, or effort to help others, he experiences a different kind of satisfaction. It creates a feeling that his life has value and purpose beyond personal gain. Even small actions like guiding someone, solving a problem, or supporting others can create a strong positive impact. This not only improves other people's lives but also builds a sense of pride and meaning within the person himself.

Inner satisfaction comes when a person feels peaceful and content with his actions and decisions. It is not dependent on outside approval or comparison with others. When a person lives according to his values and does meaningful work, he feels stable and confident from inside. This reduces stress and unnecessary pressure. He stops chasing things that do not matter and focuses on what truly brings happiness and balance in life.

With regular focus on growth, contribution, and inner satisfaction, a person builds a fulfilling and meaningful life. His happiness becomes stable, his mindset becomes strong, and his actions become purposeful. This understanding helps him stay grounded, focused, and positive while moving forward and creating a life that feels truly complete and satisfying

Building Strong, Meaningful Relationships That Support Your Purpose and Growth

Richard started his business journey with a clear goal, but he soon understood that success is not possible alone. He realized that building strong and meaningful relationships is very important for growth. In the beginning, he focused on creating genuine connections with people instead of only thinking about profit. He treated clients, partners, and team members with respect and honesty. This helped him build trust, and people started seeing him as reliable and professional. His approach was simple, he believed that good relationships create long-term success.

As Richard continued his work, he made sure to maintain these relationships by clear communication and support. He listened carefully to others' ideas and problems, and he tried to provide value in every interaction. Instead of using people for short-term benefit, he focused on mutual growth. This mindset helped him build strong connections that supported his business. People were willing to work with him again and again because they felt respected and understood. This created stability and continuous opportunities in his journey.

These relationships also helped Richard grow as a person. By interacting with different people, he learned new ideas, improved his thinking, and became more confident in handling situations. He understood the importance of teamwork and cooperation. When challenges came, his network supported him with guidance and solutions. This made him stronger and more prepared for future growth. His success was not only based on his skills but also on the strong relationships he built over time.

With consistent effort, Richard created a network of meaningful relationships that supported his purpose and growth. His business expanded, his confidence increased, and his journey became more stable. This shows that strong relationships are not just helpful, they are necessary for long-term success. A person who builds genuine connections creates a powerful foundation for growth, trust, and meaningful achievements in life

Living with Clear Vision, Strong Decisions, and a Life That Feels Truly Meaningful

When a person has a clear vision, his life gets a proper direction and purpose. He knows what he wants to achieve and why it is important for him. This clarity removes confusion and helps him focus on the right path. Instead of wasting time on unnecessary things, he uses his energy on actions that move him closer to his goals. A clear vision acts like a guide that helps him stay steady even when situations are uncertain or challenging.

Strong decisions come naturally when vision is clear. A person does not feel confused or influenced by others because he already knows what is right for him. He takes responsibility for his choices and acts with confidence. This reduces mistakes and helps him move forward with stability. When decisions are based on clear thinking and purpose, they bring better results and create a strong foundation for growth. This also builds self-trust, which is very important for long-term success.

Living with meaning is not about big achievements only, it is about feeling satisfied with daily actions. When a person's vision and decisions are aligned with his values, he feels peaceful and fulfilled. He does not compare his life with others because he knows his own journey. This mindset helps him stay positive and focused. It also reduces stress because his actions are clear and meaningful instead of random or forced.

With consistent clarity and strong decisions, a person builds a life that feels complete and purposeful. His actions create real progress, his mindset stays stable, and his confidence continues to grow. This approach helps him move forward with direction and create a life that is not only successful but also meaningful and deeply satisfying

15.

Dreams into Reality

Turning Your Vision into a Clear Goal That Guides Your Actions Every Day

Robert always had a dream of building something meaningful in his life, but for many years his vision was not clear. He wanted success, but he did not know exactly what to do every day to achieve it. One day, he decided to sit quietly and think deeply about what he truly wanted. He wrote down his vision in simple words and then converted it into clear and practical goals. This small step changed everything because now he had direction. Instead of guessing, he knew what actions to take daily, and this gave him clarity and confidence.

After setting clear goals, Robert started planning his daily routine based on those goals. He did not try to do everything at once, but focused on small tasks that were connected to his vision. Every day he completed these tasks with discipline, even when he did not feel motivated. This consistency helped him build strong habits.

Slowly, his actions started creating visible progress. He realized that clear goals make work easier because the mind knows exactly where to focus. This removed confusion and helped him use his time wisely.

There were times when Robert felt tired or faced difficulties, but his clear goals kept him on track. Whenever he felt distracted, he reminded himself of his vision and checked if his current actions were helping him move forward. This habit helped him stay focused and avoid wasting time. He also reviewed his progress regularly and made small improvements in his plan. This made his journey more organized and practical. He understood that success is not about big steps, but about daily clear actions.

With time, Robert's life became more structured and meaningful. His confidence increased because he was taking the right steps every day. His vision was no longer just a dream, it became a reality through clear goals and consistent action. This shows that when a person converts vision into clear goals, he gains direction, focus, and control over his life. It helps him move forward with purpose and build a successful and meaningful journey step by step

Combining Focused Mindset, Smart Planning, and Consistent Effort for Real Results

Robert understood that having a goal is not enough if the mind is not focused. In the beginning, he used to get distracted easily and his efforts did not give strong results. Then he decided to train his mind to stay focused on one task at a time. He removed unnecessary distractions and gave full attention to his work. This focused mindset helped him improve the quality of his actions. He realized that when the mind is clear and steady, even simple work gives better results. This became the first step in building real progress.

After improving his focus, Robert started working on smart planning. Instead of working randomly, he began to plan his tasks in a clear and practical way. He divided big goals into small steps and gave proper time to each task. This made his work more organized and less stressful. He also started thinking before taking action, which helped him avoid mistakes and save time. Smart planning helped him stay prepared and gave him confidence because he knew what to do next at every stage.

Consistency was the most important part of Robert's journey. Even on days when he felt tired or unmotivated, he continued doing his work. He did not wait for perfect mood or conditions. This habit of regular effort helped him build discipline. Slowly, his small actions started creating strong results. He understood that success does not come from one big effort, but from continuous small efforts done with focus and planning. This changed his approach completely and made him more serious about his work.

With time, the combination of focused mindset, smart planning, and consistent effort brought real and visible results in Robert's life. His progress became steady, his confidence increased, and his work started giving better outcomes. He learned that when these three things work together, they create a powerful system for success. This approach helped him move forward with clarity and build a meaningful and successful journey through discipline and right action

Taking Small but Powerful Steps Daily That Slowly Build Big Success

Robert always believed that success comes from big actions, but he often felt overwhelmed and delayed his work. One day, he changed his approach and decided to focus on small daily steps instead of waiting for the perfect moment. He started with simple tasks that were easy to complete but directly connected to his goals. This helped him take action without fear or pressure. Slowly, he understood that even small steps, when taken regularly, create real progress. This change made his journey simple and more manageable.

As Robert continued this habit, he noticed that small actions were building strong discipline in his life. Every day he completed his planned tasks without skipping, even if they looked small. This consistency increased his confidence because he was moving forward daily. He stopped worrying about how big his goal was and focused only on what he needed to do today. This mindset reduced stress and helped him stay calm and focused on his journey.

There were times when results were not visible, but Robert did not stop. He trusted his daily process and continued putting effort step by step. After some time, he started seeing the results of his consistent work. His skills improved, his work became better, and his progress became clear. He realized that success is not built in one day, it is created through daily actions that may look small but carry strong impact over time. This understanding gave him patience and belief in his process.

With regular effort, Robert's small steps turned into big achievements. His life became more organized, his focus became strong, and his growth became steady. He proved to himself that consistent daily action is more powerful than occasional big effort. This approach helped him build a successful and meaningful journey step by step with clarity and confidence

Tracking Your Progress to Stay Aware, Improve, and Move in the Right Direction

Robert was working hard every day, but for a long time he did not see clear results because he was not tracking his progress. He used to stay busy but did not know if his actions were taking him closer to his goal. One day, he decided to start writing down his daily work and checking what he completed and what he missed. This simple habit made a big difference. He became more aware of how he was using his time and where he needed improvement. This awareness helped him take better control of his actions.

As Robert continued tracking his progress, he started noticing patterns in his work. He found out which tasks were helping him grow and which activities were wasting his time. This helped him remove unnecessary work and focus only on important tasks. He also began setting small targets and checking them regularly. This made his work more organized and gave him a clear direction. Tracking helped him stay honest with himself because he could clearly see his effort and results.

This habit also helped Robert improve continuously. When he saw his mistakes or missed tasks, he did not feel discouraged. Instead, he used that information to make better plans for the next day. He started adjusting his routine based on what worked and what did not. This made his progress steady and strong. He learned that improvement is only possible when a person is aware of his actions and ready to make changes. This mindset helped him grow faster and more effectively.

With time, tracking progress became a powerful tool in Robert's journey. It kept him focused, disciplined, and aware of his direction. His confidence increased because he could see his growth clearly. This habit helped him stay on the right path and avoid confusion. It proved that when a person tracks his progress regularly, he moves forward with clarity, improves his performance, and builds a strong and successful journey step by step

Facing Challenges with Courage and Using Them as Stepping Stones for Growth

Robert faced many challenges when he started working toward his goals. There were timcs when things did not go as planned, and he felt pressure and doubt. In the beginning, he used to avoid difficult situations, but he soon realized that avoiding problems only delays progress. He decided to face challenges with courage instead of fear. This change in thinking helped him become mentally stronger. He understood that challenges are not there to stop him, but to teach him something important and prepare him for bigger responsibilities.

As Robert started facing challenges directly, he began learning valuable lessons from each situation. Every problem helped him improve his skills, thinking, and decision making. When he made mistakes, he did not feel ashamed, instead he tried to understand what went wrong and how he could do better next time. This attitude turned his failures into learning opportunities. He slowly started seeing challenges as stepping stones that were helping him move forward instead of holding him back.

This approach also increased Robert's confidence and problem-solving ability. Each time he handled a difficult situation, he felt more capable and strong. He stopped depending on others for every solution and started trusting his own thinking. This made him more independent and responsible. He learned to stay calm during tough situations and focus on finding solutions instead of worrying about the problem. This mindset helped him handle pressure in a better way.

With continuous effort and courage, Robert turned his challenges into powerful growth opportunities. His mindset became positive, his actions became stronger, and his journey became more meaningful. He proved that when a person faces difficulties with courage and uses them to learn, he builds a strong foundation for success. This approach helps in growing step by step and creates a path that leads to confidence, stability, and real achievement

Staying Consistent and Motivated Even When Progress Feels Slow

Robert was working hard every day, but there was a time when he felt that his progress was very slow. He was putting effort, but results were not visible quickly. This made him feel frustrated and confused. Many times, he thought about stopping, but then he reminded himself why he started. He understood that slow progress does not mean no progress. This thought helped him stay calm and continue his work with patience. He decided that he would not depend on quick results to stay motivated, but on his daily commitment.

To stay consistent, Robert focused on building a simple routine. He fixed a time for his important work and followed it daily without excuses. Even on days when he did not feel motivated, he still completed his tasks. He understood that motivation comes and goes, but consistency is a choice. This mindset helped him continue his efforts without depending on mood. Slowly, his discipline became strong, and his work started improving step by step.

Robert also learned to find motivation in small achievements. Instead of waiting for big success, he started appreciating his daily progress. Completing small tasks gave him a sense of satisfaction and kept his energy positive. He stopped comparing himself with others and focused only on his own journey. This reduced pressure and helped him stay focused. He realized that staying consistent is more important than being perfect.

With time, Robert's slow progress turned into strong results. His efforts started showing, and his confidence increased. He understood that success comes from regular action, even when results are not immediate. His journey became stable and meaningful because he did not give up during slow phases. This shows that when a person stays consistent and keeps himself motivated, he builds a strong path toward success with patience and determination

Learning from Every Experience and Using It to Become Stronger and Wiser

Robert's journey was full of different experiences, some were good and some were difficult. In the beginning, he used to feel upset when things did not go his way, but slowly he understood that every experience has something to teach. He started observing his actions and results carefully. Instead of blaming situations or people, he began asking himself what he could learn from each situation. This simple habit changed his mindset and helped him grow in a better way.

Whenever Robert made a mistake, he did not try to hide it or ignore it. He accepted it and tried to understand the reason behind it. This helped him avoid repeating the same mistakes again. Good experiences also became a source of learning because he understood what worked well and how he could use it again. This made his thinking more practical and clear. He realized that learning is not only from books but also from real-life situations that happen daily.

This approach made Robert mentally stronger and wiser. He became calm in difficult situations because he knew that every challenge carries a lesson. He stopped fearing failure and started seeing it as a part of growth. This helped him take better decisions and handle problems with confidence. His understanding of life improved, and he became more patient and focused. This inner growth helped him move forward without losing direction.

With time, Robert's habit of learning from every experience made his journey more meaningful and powerful. He kept improving himself step by step and became stronger with each situation. His confidence increased because he trusted his learning process. This shows that when a person learns from every experience and uses it wisely, he grows continuously and builds a strong and successful life with knowledge and understanding

Achieving Your Goals and Expanding Your Vision to Create an Even Greater Future

Robert worked with full focus and consistency for many months, and finally he started achieving his goals one by one. These achievements gave him confidence and satisfaction, but he did not stop there. He understood that success is not a final point, it is a continuous journey. After reaching his first goals, he took time to reflect on what he had learned and how he had grown. This reflection helped him see bigger possibilities for his future. His vision started expanding because now he believed more in his abilities.

Instead of becoming comfortable, Robert used his success as a base to aim higher. He started setting new and bigger goals that challenged him to grow further. His thinking became broader, and he began to explore new opportunities. He understood that growth comes when a person pushes his limits and moves beyond his comfort zone. This mindset helped him stay motivated and excited about his journey. He did not fear bigger goals because his past experience gave him confidence.

As Robert expanded his vision, he also improved his planning and actions. He became more focused and clear about what he wanted to achieve next. He used his past learning to make better decisions and avoid mistakes. This made his progress more stable and strong. He also started thinking about how his work could create a bigger impact. This shift from small thinking to big vision helped him grow not only in success but also in purpose.

With time, Robert built a future that was bigger and more meaningful than he had imagined earlier. His journey did not stop after achieving one goal, it kept moving forward with new vision and stronger actions. This shows that when a person achieves his goals and then expands his vision, he creates continuous growth and new opportunities. It helps him build a powerful future with confidence, clarity, and a strong sense of purpose

Discipline and Motivational Lines

1. I can do it
2. I will achieve my goals
3. I am becoming successful
4. I believe in myself
5. I am strong and focused
6. I never give up
7. I am improving every day
8. I take action without fear
9. I am confident in my journey
10. I create my own success
11. I stay disciplined in my work
12. I learn from every mistake
13. I am growing step by step
14. I trust my decisions
15. I stay calm in every situation
16. I move forward with clarity
17. I control my thoughts
18. I attract positive results
19. I am building my future
20. I stay committed to my goals
21. I use my time wisely

22. I am focused on my path
23. I believe in my dreams
24. I turn challenges into opportunities
25. I am becoming better every day
26. I take responsibility for my life
27. I stay positive and strong
28. I handle pressure with confidence
29. I create opportunities for myself
30. I work hard with smart planning
31. I stay motivated daily
32. I follow my purpose
33. I build strong habits
34. I respect my time and effort
35. I stay patient and consistent
36. I overcome every obstacle
37. I am in control of my life
38. I think clearly and act wisely
39. I trust the process of growth
40. I am capable of great success
41. I stay focused on what matters
42. I make progress every day
43. I turn my vision into reality

44. I am disciplined and determined
45. I believe success is mine
46. I take small steps with confidence
47. I stay strong in tough times
48. I am creating a meaningful life
49. I achieve what I start
50. I am unstoppable

www.ingramcontent.com/pod-product-compliance
Lightning Source LLC
Chambersburg PA
CBHW031522180726
48282CB00056B/204
* 9 7 8 9 3 5 7 8 2 1 4 8 3 *